CROSSROADS
OF DECISION

Howard Jablon

CROSSROADS OF DECISION

The State Department and Foreign Policy, 1933-1937

THE UNIVERSITY PRESS OF KENTUCKY

Copyright © 1983 by The University Press of Kentucky

Scholarly publisher for the Commonwealth,
serving Bellarmine College, Berea College, Centre
College of Kentucky, Eastern Kentucky University,
The Filson Club, Georgetown College, Kentucky
Historical Society, Kentucky State University,
Morehead State University, Murray State University,
Northern Kentucky University, Transylvania University,
University of Kentucky, University of Louisville,
and Western Kentucky University.

Editorial and Sales Offices: Lexington, Kentucky 40506-0024

Library of Congress Cataloging in Publication Data

Jablon, Howard.
    Crossroads of decision.

    Bibliography: p.
    Includes index.
    1. United States. Dept. of State.   2. United
States—Foreign policy—1933-1945.   I. Title.
JX1706.A4 1983c   353.1   82-40459
ISBN 0-8131-1483-7

Contents

For my children
Lisa and Erica

Preface

In his memoirs, former Secretary of State Cordell Hull states
that in 1934 the United States was at the "Oriental crossroads of decision." One road led to acquiescence to Japanese
expansion. The other road led to resisting that expansion,
with force if necessary. Hull remembers why he and President Roosevelt chose the second road. But Hull's recollection
of the events of 1934 was faulty. He and his colleagues in the
State Department did not advise curtailing Japanese ambitions. Instead, they merely continued the policy of nonrecognition and espoused the ideals of the Open Door. That
approach achieved nothing.

Nevertheless, Hull's memory serves us well by reminding
us of the critical nature of decision making in the early New
Deal period. The United States was at a crossroads where
many policy decisions intersected. The country had to select
the appropriate direction for American policy in Europe,
Latin America, and Africa, as well as the Orient. Crises
occurred in each area that presented the Roosevelt administration with difficult choices. Selecting the appropriate path
was made more arduous by the overriding need for the new
administration to rehabilitate a devastated economy at
home.

During the early New Deal period, from 1933 to 1937, the
State Department assisted Roosevelt in the formulation of
foreign policy decisions. At that time, the department enjoyed greater influence than it was to have later on when
Roosevelt participated more directly in foreign affairs.[1] For
the most part, its influence was not beneficial. The depart-

ment stubbornly adhered to principles or universal formulas or doctrines that did not fit the demands of particular situations. The Open Door policy, the Good Neighbor policy, the Reciprocal Trade Agreement program, the nonrecognition doctrine, neutrality, and noninterference all failed in one way or another to achieve the lofty goals they were supposed to achieve. There was, moreover, an excessive reliance on diplomatic techniques: signing treaties, reaching agreements, attending international meetings, and extending or withholding recognition of governments. In short, there is nothing to suggest that the State Department, despite its impressive array of professional diplomats and technical advisers, possessed any greater wisdom than the president.

To date, little has been written on the influence of the State Department on New Deal diplomacy. We have studies like Robert Dallek's, which survey the entire era from a presidential perspective, or studies that deal with single problems, like Robert A. Divine's work on neutrality and Armin Rappaport's and Dorothy Borg's on the bilateral relationship with Japan.[2] The only work on the State Department is Herbert Feis's *1933*, a generally favorable account of the department's work during that critical year.[3]

Like Feis, I believe that 1933 was an important year in foreign affairs as well as domestic. Unlike Feis, I have not limited the study to one year but have extended it to 1937, when Roosevelt began to take direct control of foreign policy. I also emphasize different aspects of the department in that period. Whereas Feis concentrates on personalities and events, I concentrate on ideas and policy. Furthermore, I disagree with his favorable interpretation, and I present a critical view of the recommendations the department made.

At the outset, I want to express my gratitude to those people who, in one way or another, made the completion of this book possible.

At Rutgers University I was fortunate in having two men with entirely different viewpoints supervise my work. The late L. Ethan Ellis's seminar in the diplomacy of the 1930s was an exercise in the Rankian school of writing *wie es eigentlich gewesen.* Later, I learned from Lloyd Gardner to appreciate history as Lord Acton described it: as "the record of truths revealed by experience . . . [and] an instrument of action and power that goes to the making of the future."

Good criticism is often difficult to find, and I consider myself very fortunate in having received the comments of several knowledgeable readers. Warren Sussman read the initial draft of this book. Wayne Cole subsequently corrected some flaws in my approach to the arms embargo controversy. Harold Hyman patiently sorted out both substantive and stylistic errors as the work neared completion.

I am also indebted to the staffs of the Franklin D. Roosevelt Library, the Houghton Library of Harvard University, the Hoover Institution of Stanford University, the Yale University Library, the manuscript division of the Library of Congress, and the National Archives. I appreciate the opportunity I had to read the manuscripts under their care.

Two journals, *Mid-America* and *The Historian,* graciously allowed me to include in this book two articles I had written and they had published. Chapter 4 is based on my article "Cordell Hull, His 'Associates,' And Relations With Japan, 1933-1936," *Mid-America* 56, no. 3 (July 1974): 160-74. Chapter 5 is based on my article "The State Department and Collective Security, 1933-34," *The Historian* 33, no. 2 (February 1971), 248-63.

Marlene Bennett, an extraordinary typist, created order out of chaos. My colleagues, Sally Black and John Pappas, proofread the book and made it even more orderly.

We were now at the Oriental crossroads of decision. There were two courses open to us. One was to withdraw gradually, perhaps with dignity, from the Far East. This meant acquiescence in the nullification of our treaty rights, the closing of the Open Door, further Japanese appropriation of pieces of China and other territory, relinquishing the protection of our citizens and abandoning them to unequal competition with Japanese-operated monopolies. . . .

The other course was to continue to insist on the maintenance of law, on our legitimate rights and interests in the Far East, and on observance of the treaties and declarations that guaranteed an independent China and pledged equality to all nations, nonintervention, nonaggression, and peaceful settlement of disputes in the Orient. This meant a firm, though not an aggressive, policy toward Japan, especially in the light of her evident plans of territorial expansion by force. It meant adequate military preparedness. . . .

The President and I chose the second course.

CORDELL HULL

1. The Economics of an Old Deal

Herbert Feis, the economic adviser of the State Department in both the Hoover and Roosevelt administrations, recalls how the presence of the Bonus Expeditionary Force in Washington in 1932 dramatized the sad economic plight of the country.[1] That summer World War I veterans went to Washington to lobby for a bill providing payment of war service bonuses. The veterans built a shantytown on Anacostia Flats. When they ran out of space, they squatted on land and in unused government buildings on Pennsylvania Avenue. The Senate refused to approve the bonus bill, and about half of the Bonus Force went home, leaving five or six thousand veterans. For a time Brigadier General Pelham D. Glassford handled the group with dignity and composure. Unfortunately, President Herbert Hoover was less patient. The administration ordered the veterans removed from the buildings, and a confrontation occurred on July 28 in which two veterans were killed. Convinced the skirmish was part of a communist-gangster plot, Hoover authorized General Douglas MacArthur to disperse the veterans. Regular troops did so with tanks, tear gas, and bayonets. The incident dramatized the extent and danger of the economic collapse, but many officials remained optimistic that it would soon improve.

Feis claims to have been more pessimistic and more perceptive than his colleagues about the deep-seated nature of the depression and its possibly dangerous international consequences. His gloomy prognostications earned him a reputation in the department as a prophet of doom. His lack of optimism, however, was justified. Feis was not reassured when President Hoover insisted that the depression was the result of the economic policies of other countries and maintained that a high tariff was necessary to protect the United States from further troubles. Hoover ignored the claims of leaders of European countries who charged that their economic problems stemmed largely from the depression in the United States and the country's insistence on collection of the World War I debts. Feis observed that on this issue the president displayed some agility in both speech and logic when he simultaneously promised no cancellation of the debts but suggested canceling installments if the United States were compensated by increased purchases of its goods.[2] Hoover continued to hold to his international view of the causes of the depression, and after his defeat urged the incoming administration to look abroad for a solution to the economic disaster.[3]

Roosevelt rejected Hoover's interpretation that the economic malaise was imported. But, aside from criticizing the Hoover policies, he offered no real alternative. At one point he suggested that trade barriers be lowered. Later he reversed himself and promised a tariff high enough to prevent competition to American products. His ambiguity may have reflected a split in his party; some Democrats were fervent supporters of international cooperation, but others, advocating a high tariff, were zealous in their conviction that the American government should do what was necessary without regard for the effect on other nations.[4] Roosevelt's advisers disagreed as to whether to expand trade by lowering tariffs immediately or to maintain tariffs until the domestic economic crisis abated. Hull advocated immediate reduction whereas Raymond Moley, one of Roosevelt's Brain Trust, argued for postponing the reduction.[5]

Of the members of Roosevelt's new administration, Hull stands out as an advocate of economic internationalism. From the beginning of his political life as a congressman from Tennessee, he championed low tariff policies. He ob-

jected to the political implications of high tariffs, which he
believed would "enable a few thousand manufacturers to sell
their products to the people at more than a reasonable and
fair profit."[6] Hull saw economic virtue in lower tariffs as
part of an effort to open foreign markets. Although indus-
trial and financial development at home would continue, he
maintained that the country should concentrate on expansion beyond the seas. Hull's concern about tariffs tran-
scended their domestic effect; he believed protectionism had
adverse international effects. In 1916, he sponsored a joint
resolution requesting the eventual meeting of an international trade conference in Washington at which the commercial nations of the world would establish a permanent
trade-agreement congress. The congress would consider unfair trade practices and formulate agreements to eliminate
them. At the end of World War I he continued to support
such an approach. He was convinced that the war had resulted from economic tension between the major trading
nations of the world. He endorsed the third of Wilson's Fourteen Points, which called for removal of trade restrictions
and promotion of commercial equality.[7] His conviction that
freer trade would promote peace became central to his policies as secretary of state.

Hull's analyses matured at the height of the Progressive
movement and during the world war, when idealism flourished. Perhaps such views were to be expected from an inex-
perienced congressman, but he tenaciously held to them for
the remainder of his public career. In the 1920s and 1930s
he argued for lower tariffs, attacking Republican protection-
ist policies. For example, he criticized the 1922 Fordney-
McCumber tariff, which he believed violated his economic
principles, and he urged a commercial policy that looked to
modest revenues and the removal of barriers to cooperation.[8] And in 1931 he asked that the country take the lead
in an international movement to eliminate tariff barriers
gradually. He repeated a suggestion similar to the one he
had made in 1916 to establish a permanent world economic
conference for the promotion of liberal trade policies and

elimination of unfair practices that caused strife. Hull's record on the tariff issue could have left no doubt as to how he wanted the new administration to view the depression and international relations.

Because Hull had had no previous diplomatic experience, he knew he would need to depend upon career officers. Indeed, before accepting the position of secretary of state, he stipulated that the undersecretary should have considerable experience. Roosevelt concurred and selected William Phillips, a career officer with a distinguished record. Although there were no serious tensions between Hull and Phillips, their differing temperaments and the undersecretary's long friendship with Roosevelt caused some discomfort. Nevertheless, Hull leaned on Phillips and other officers in the department, including Herbert Feis and Stanley K. Hornbeck.

Years later Hull recalled that when he undertook running the State Department he made clear to Roosevelt that he "would not be a mere transmitter and receiver of messages to and from foreign Governments" and that he would have a "full share in formulating and carrying out foreign policy."[9] During the early New Deal, Hull recalled, Roosevelt was too busy with domestic affairs to direct foreign policy, and the secretary had a great deal of freedom. To some extent that observation is true. But as the events surrounding the World Monetary and Economic Conference in London in 1933 demonstrate, Hull had an extremely difficult time with one of his subordinates, Assistant Secretary Raymond Moley, with some members of the delegation to the conference, and especially with Roosevelt. Thus the significance of the conference, aside from its immediate import, was whether or not Hull would exercise a decisive role in evolving the international economic policy of the new administration.

The 1933 World Monetary and Economic Conference was convened in response to the debts and reparation issues. By 1931 the matter of the payments of the World War I debts to the United States by the Entente powers, which had been linked to the Entente's collection of reparations from Germany, reached a critical point as the worldwide depression made liquidating the debts impossible. Hoover responded to the crisis by suspending collection on debts owed to the United States for one year with the understanding that the victors would suspend their collection of reparations for the same period. That grace period, the Hoover Moratorium, was set to expire on December 15, 1932, prompting the debtor nations to meet at Lausanne in June 1932. At that conference the participating states agreed to cancel German reparations. In addition to the Lausanne accord, an understanding was concluded at that June meeting between Great Britain, France, Belgium, and Italy which provided that the accord on reparations was not to come into effect until these nations arrived at a satisfactory settlement with their major creditor, the United States.

In May 1931, thirteen months before the Lausanne meeting, the British ambassador to the United States, Sir Ronald Lindsay, questioned Undersecretary William R. Castle, Jr., about the possibility of United States participation in a world economic conference. The ambassador intimated that the conference would be a sequel to the Lausanne meeting on reparations. President Hoover showed interest in the proposal because he was convinced that the economic dislocation in America was the result of developments in Europe and because he thought the conference would have some psychological and domestic political benefit. It would also offer a way to mollify senators agitating for an international meeting on silver. But Hoover imposed severe restrictions on American participation: the United States would not discuss debts or specific tariff rates, and something had to be done to help the silver industry.[10]

Secretary of State Henry L. Stimson relayed these limitations to Feis and asked him to prepare a memorandum indicating what might be accomplished if such a conference were held under the limitations imposed by the president. Feis's reply was terse: "It seems to me that the proposed conference could achieve nothing important *except possibly in one direction* . . . a devaluation of gold—that is, a reduction of the number of grains of gold metal corresponding to the dollar and other units of currency. These measures might give increased place to silver in the monetary sphere."[11] Stimson was not pleased with Feis's comments. He thought that the economic adviser had taken the president's limitations too seriously and had handled his assignment as though it were routine rather than urgent. Stimson noted that Hoover was desperate for solutions. Feis replied that none could be found to fit the president's conceptions.[12]

Stimson could not persuade Hoover to remove any of the conditions but wrote to British Prime Minister Ramsay MacDonald on May 25, outlining what a conference might accomplish. Joint actions could raise commodity prices and encourage private economic groups throughout the world by demonstrating that governments were trying to find a common way of solving problems. Another result, Stimson added, might be to bring order into currency relationships. The secretary suggested the conference be held in London because the British had already gone off the gold standard. If the United States were to host the meeting, additional speculation might be set off about American policy that would further disturb the monetary situation. Finally, Stimson suggested that the conference bring together the heads of state, after suitable preliminary discussion and preparation.[13]

In 1932 steps were taken to convene the economic conference. Two planning groups were created: an organizing committee and a commission of experts. The issue of American representation on these groups immediately set off a dispute between the State Department and Secretary of the Treasury Ogden Mills, who wanted to make sure that his views were represented. He recommended the selection of the American ambassador to London, Andrew Mellon, his predecessor as secretary of the treasury. In that office Mellon had advocated balancing the budget, paying off the debt, and at the same time reducing taxes for the higher brackets. Feis and other members of the State Department found Mellon's views objectionable and argued that most European govern-

ments believed he represented practices that were in disre-
pute.[14] The effect of their advice is debatable, though
Stimson selected Norman H. Davis and Frederic M. Sackett,
not Mellon, to serve on the organizing committee. Davis, a
Democrat, was not the favored choice of partisan Republi-
cans and isolationist Democrats, who opposed his interna-
tionalist views.

For the preparatory commission of experts two United
States representatives were needed, one to deal with financial questions and the other with economic questions. The
secretary of the treasury wanted Professor John H. Williams
of Harvard, because Williams advocated that countries off
the gold standard, particularly Great Britain, should return
to that standard. No one in the department objected to this
choice, but controversy arose over selection of the other
member of the preparatory commission. Mills wanted Julius
Klein, the assistant secretary of commerce, but the State
Department considered him so incompetent that Hoover selected Edmund Day, director for the social sciences of the
Rockefeller Foundation.[15]

The experts met in Geneva in October and agreed on lines
of action but could not agree on the relative importance of
these lines. Most of the members agreed that Britain and
Japan should return to the gold standard at set rates for
their currencies. But representatives from these countries
argued that their domestic situations were cloudy and that
any decision on stabilization had to await improvement in
their debt situation and an expansion of trade and prices.
Nevertheless, when the American experts submitted their
report to Washington, Stimson optimistically believed that
some agreement could be reached. Mills, on the other hand,
was pleased with Williams's stand on the importance of stabilization but was skeptical about the ability of the conference to come to decisions.[16]

After the Democratic victory in the autumn election, the
question emerged whether Roosevelt would endorse the
proposed conference. In the interval between Roosevelt's
election and inauguration, the State Department tried to
maintain a liaison between Hoover and Roosevelt on three

matters: the economic conference, the debt question, and
Japan's activity in Manchuria. With the possible exception
of the discussions on the Far East, attempts at coordination
failed. With respect to the conference, the only significant
outcome was the decision that the United States would participate as soon as possible after the Roosevelt administration entered office.[17]

Soon after Roosevelt's inauguration on March 4, 1933, the
president suggested to the British ambassador that the
prime minister visit Washington. Ambassador Sir Ronald
Lindsay told Roosevelt that MacDonald would come only if
war debts were discussed. Roosevelt replied, "Why shouldn't
he come and talk debts?" Feis, among others, was skeptical
that any agreements could be reached at a meeting between
Roosevelt and the prime minister. More serious, he felt,
was the possibility that if the heads of government disagreed, their disagreement might jeopardize the economic
conference. Nevertheless, invitations to come to Washington were also extended to France, Canada, Italy, Germany, Brazil, Japan, and Chile. Nothing came out of these
side meetings except the decisions to open the conference
in London on June 12 and that heads of state would not
attend.[18]

At the time of the conference Roosevelt was giving consideration to the stabilization of the dollar. According to Feis,
"It was hard to tell what the President wanted. His ideas
veered and waffled." Roosevelt led the British and French
missions to believe that stabilization of the dollar was possible. In his message on May 16 to the World Disarmament
Conference then in progress in Geneva, he had expressed a
belief that the economic conference "must establish order in
place of the present chaos by a stabilization of currencies, by
freeing the flow of world trade, and by international action
to raise price levels." Yet within two weeks of that message
Roosevelt decided that the conference should not discuss
stabilization. Cordell Hull was relieved. Either he was unin-
terested or he suspected that the issue would invite trouble.
In the instructions to the American delegation to the confer-

ence he focused only on a resolution to reduce trade restrictions and end exchange controls as fast as possible.[19]

On the eve of departure for London Hull did not appear disturbed because Raymond Moley stayed behind to act as liaison between the delegation and the president, even though Moley believed that domestic economic rehabilitation must precede international agreements. On May 20 Moley had delivered a speech warning that "action of an international conference which attempted to bring about cures for these [economic] difficulties solely by concerted international measures would necessarily result in failure."[20] Nor did Hull appear distraught over the delegation Roosevelt had selected, which left him as chairman with only one ally outside the State Department experts accompanying him, Governor James M. Cox, the Democratic presidential candidate in 1920 and the vice-chairman of the delegation. Other delegates, who were not sympathetic to Hull's views, included Key Pittman, chairman of the Senate Foreign Relations Committee; James Couzens, allegedly the only Republican senator willing to go to London; Samuel D. McReynolds, chairman of the House Foreign Affairs Committee; and Ralph W. Morrison, a wealthy Texan selected for political reasons.[21]

Hull finally came face to face with reality on the trip to London. Roosevelt informed him that he would not ask Congress for a new tariff. Apparently the president was responding to a State Department effort to draft legislation that would authorize the president to negotiate with other nations to effect a mutual reduction in tariff rates and enter into reciprocity agreements with other countries for lower trade restrictions. Hull immediately called Roosevelt, pleading for reconsideration in view of the reaction of other nations. Although Roosevelt expressed sympathy, he responded that it was not only inadvisable but politically impossible to take action on the tariff. Hull was disappointed, a feeling shared by experts from the department who accompanied him.[22] Plans for the conference had to be changed.

Just before the conference began, Hull was worried because Roosevelt's attitude meant an end to any effort to reach an agreement on tariff reduction, Hull's grand design for world peace and prosperity. Cox and William C. Bullitt tried to revive the secretary's spirit. They persuaded Roosevelt to send words of encouragement. But it was evident that when Hull addressed the conference on June 13 calling for a reduction in trade barriers and for international monetary stability he had been virtually abandoned by the president.[23]

Off to a bad start, the conference deteriorated rapidly. Violent disagreement erupted in the American delegation. Feis and other advisers put together a list of topics dealing with international trade for the conference to consider. It included a recommendation to discuss a 10 percent cut in all tariffs. Feis presented the proposal to the secretariat of the conference with Hull's approval. Senator Pittman was infuriated and promptly issued a press statement denying that the American delegation was supporting any such proposal. On June 18, when the delegation next met, Pittman vilified Feis, who answered in kind and said that he wished to resign. After the meeting, Hull prevailed upon Feis to remain. But anger lingered, and soon after that exchange Pittman, presumably drunk, chased Feis with a hunting knife down the corridor of their hotel. Fortunately, the senator was subdued by his friend (guardian), Ned Bruce, who was in London to protect Pittman from harming himself and others.[24]

A short time later Moley arrived in London. What he was supposed to accomplish is still unclear, but it appears that he believed he might rescue the conference and turn it from the path proposed by the internationalists.[25] Before leaving for London, Moley had discussed monetary stabilization with Roosevelt, and the decision had been made to keep stabilization off the agenda.

The president also sent Professor Oliver M. W. Sprague of Harvard and George L. Harrison, governor of the New York Federal Reserve Bank, to discuss the issue of stabilization with the British and French delegations at the conference in separate meetings. The two men had no instructions, but

Sprague was told to try to obtain an arrangement to assist monetary exchanges. In London these representatives reached agreement on temporary stabilization among the three nations. Sprague and Harrison urged the president to accept the proposal, but he declined and instructed Sprague and Harrison to concern themselves only with permanent worldwide stabilization. When other delegations, including the Hull delegation, learned about the separate meetings and Roosevelt's position, all discussion about stabilization bogged down.

Roosevelt apparently wanted Moley to work out an arrangement to soothe the gold bloc countries and steady the dollar, so long as it did not result in a loss of gold or stop price advances in the United States. But how this was to be accomplished was a mystery. Moley was given no specific instructions. He interpreted Roosevelt's wishes to mean that he was the president's envoy, bringing the delegation firsthand news about developments in Washington and the latest word on Roosevelt's views. But because Roosevelt had not made any of this clear to anyone, Hull viewed Moley's actions in London as insubordination. To make matters worse, Moley's conduct was high-handed to the point of arrogance.[26]

From the day he arrived in London, Moley clashed with Hull and members of the delegation. Hull chastised him for trying to create the impression that he was the savior of the conference. Moley protested that his mission was in keeping with his previous understanding with Hull that his objectives were limited to a liaison rule that he had announced in New York and on arrival in England. But Moley was not telling the whole truth. As the president's representative he was to discuss currency fluctuation. On June 29 he decided to investigate the circumstances surrounding a recently drawn declaration by the gold bloc countries that the British said they would sign if the United States did. Moley asked Bullitt to tell Hull that he and Sprague would handle any further discussion about currency. Apparently there were several reasons why Moley wanted to take matters into his own hands. Cox had no authority to negotiate, and Moley disliked James P. Warburg, one of the experts on monetary matters.[27] And despite his protestations to Hull, Moley wanted a set place in the conference. It was evident to him that no progress could be made without agreement on monetary matters. Undoubtedly Moley's ambition influenced Hull to concede to Moley a place in the discussion about stabilization, despite Hull's resentment of the assistant secretary's presence.

In a casual meeting on July 1 there was a serious flare-up between Moley and Hull. What prompted Hull's outburst is difficult to say. Possibly the secretary saw an opportunity to throw an anchor to a sinking enemy. The secretary accused Moley of seeking his job and subjecting him to constant humiliation.[28] And Hull had yet another opportunity to put Moley in his place. As the Hulls were about to leave for a weekend with the Astors at Cliveden, Moley sought out the secretary to express alarm at Roosevelt's possibly negative reaction to stabilization. In panic, Moley asked what to do. Hull cut him off, saying that Moley had no business in London in the first place and should go home. The secretary walked away.

On July 2 the president sent his "bombshell message," rebuking the delegation for concentrating on currency stabilization. Because the other participating nations would not agree to consider tariff reduction until after stabilization was settled, the conference staggered from the blow. Hull used the occasion to show loyalty to the president rather than to express the shock he and other members of the delegation felt. Moley was less skillful. He sent a memorandum to the president in which he recommended a two-week recess to allow Roosevelt time to prepare a resolution to present to the conference, presumably to salvage something from the wreckage. Moley went on to evaluate the members of the delegation, none of whom, he observed, except Pittman, represented Roosevelt's views. He criticized the advisers, whom Feis headed, as inordinately progressive. He concluded that another reason for a recess would be to reconstitute the delegation.[29]

After Moley left the conference, the contents of his message to Roosevelt were revealed. Hull seethed with anger at the behavior of his subordinate. He called Roosevelt on July 11, just before Moley was due to land in the United States, complaining bitterly about Moley's conduct. His agenda of grievances included hurt over Moley's profession of loyalty in London while simultaneously cabling the president to complain that Hull was incompetent. Hull's report was joined with an equally damaging statement from the American ambassador in London, Robert Bingham, who praised Hull's work as head of the delegation and cataloged Moley's misdeeds. Bingham criticized the self-aggrandizing way in which Moley advertised himself to the press as the only person who represented the president and could save the conference. He decried Moley's treachery in using the cable facilities of the embassy to send his message to the president. Bingham also reported his displeasure to two members of the president's inner circle, Colonel Edward M. House and Louis Howe, thereby assuring Roosevelt's attention.[30] The reports guaranteed an end to Moley's service in the State Department.

Meanwhile, the conference limped along with the secretary and others doing what they could to avoid its immediate collapse. Hull did have an opportunity to address the conference on trade. On July 20 he advocated reciprocal trade agreements based on the most-favored-nation principle. In the twilight of the conference he corresponded with the president about trade, and the president placated him with reassurance about their mutual interest in eliminating trade barriers.[31]

The World Monetary and Economic Conference was a failure. Nothing was accomplished toward monetary stability and, beyond offering a prayer for lower tariffs based upon a reciprocal trade program, little was done to facilitate international commerce. From the debris of blasted hopes, however, Hull formed ties with members of the department who admired his dignity in the face of adversity. These ties were strenghtened as the years progressed.[32]

Hull had another opportunity to present his economic ideas. Some months after the London conference, the United States participated in a Pan-American conference in Montevideo. Hull wanted this conference to succeed but was unsure of the prospects. Hull believed many nations, including the United States, were moving toward extreme economic nationalism.[33] Consequently, he carefully prepared the groundwork for the conference. For domestic consumption Hull offered the assurance that there was no conflict between the president's domestic emergency relief program and a permanent international economic program.[34] The program he envisioned was reflected in three resolutions he presented to the conference: one condemning discriminatory trade practices, one endorsing a tariff truce, and one encouraging multilateral trade agreements.[35]

Roosevelt conditionally supported Hull's plan for Montevideo. He told Acting Secretary Phillips that he supported the idea of liberal tariffs by combined action of many nations, as long as any agreement included safeguards to protect the domestic recovery programs for agriculture and industry. Hull was pleased with Roosevelt's response.[36]

At the conference Hull combined economics with politics. He offered an elaborate resolution that looked to reduction of trade barriers in the hemisphere, setting an example for the rest of the world. In exchange, he promised that the United States would "carry on in the spirit of that application of the Golden Rule by which we mean the true good will of the true good neighbor."[37] The artful combination of a call for more liberal trade in the hemisphere through a series of bilateral reciprocity treaties and the promise of noninterference in Latin American affairs proved irresistible to almost all the conference delegates.

The minister from Haiti, however, walked out of the meeting to protest continued United States control of Haitian customs.[38] The Haitian demonstration sparked a minor diplomatic conflagration. All the Latin American delegates were inflamed by the policies of the United States in Haiti and Cuba. Allusions were made to control of customs reve-

nues, an obvious reference to Haiti, and to the use of warships, an equally obvious reference to Cuba. Even Carlos
Saavedra Lamas, the Argentine foreign minister, who
agreed with Hull's economic policies and had promised to
come to his defense if there were an explosion, joined the
protest. At that point Hull demonstrated diplomatic finesse.
He remained quiet during the storm, and when it was over
he shook Saavedra Lamas's hand and told him he understood that he could have done nothing else under the circumstances. Saavedra Lamas was won over by the public display
of friendship and from that point supported the United
States position.[39]

Skillful diplomacy and the clever combination of the
promise to be a good neighbor and a liberal trader were
effective. On the day Hull announced the United States'
intention to be a good neighbor, the conference's committee
on economic matters unanimously adopted the tariff resolution. Hull had reason to be proud. He had succeeded in Montevideo and looked forward to the time when other nations
would follow the example of the Latin American states. His
success was enhanced by the way his victory was received in
the department. His colleagues, as Phillips noted, admired
his "unique method of diplomacy, which proves irresistible."[40]

In addition to its immediate effect, the Montevideo conference furthered the Good Neighbor policy, which had begun
when President Hoover allowed State Department official J.
Reuben Clark to publish his *Memorandum on the Monroe
Doctrine* in 1928. Clark argued that the interventionist
Roosevelt Corollary of 1904 was not a logical outgrowth of
the Monroe Doctrine. He did not deny that the United States
had the right of intervention but stated that such intervention was not sanctioned by the Monroe Doctrine. Stimson
had amplified the Hoover administration's position that the
Monroe Doctrine was a statement concerning the United
States vis-à-vis Europe, not the United States vis-à-vis Latin
America. The Good Neighbor policy emphasized dual reciprocity, assuming that if the United States gave Latin

American states what they wanted, those countries would
return the favor. Thus the "gift" of noninterference would
be reciprocated with lower tariffs. By linking reciprocal
trade agreements to the promise of political neighborliness,
Hull gave the new look an old slant. His objective was primarily economic, and until World War II the Good Neighbor
policy was the good customer campaign.[41]

Hull might have followed the advice of the ambassador to
Mexico, Josephus Daniels, who on October 17, 1933, sent a
letter to the department recommending that the United
States use the occasion of the Montevideo conference to
make a statement relating the Monroe Doctrine to the administration's Good Neighbor policy. He suggested that
President Roosevelt assure the world that the United States
claimed no right or privilege for itself in this hemisphere
which it denied to European countries and that the United
States would accept the limitation imposed on European
states not to interfere in the affairs of other states in this
hemisphere. In brief, Daniels was calling for the Pan-Americanization of the Monroe Doctrine. But this recommendation was rejected.[42]

Hull's struggle for his program of free trade did not end
at Montevideo. For the next two years the secretary battled
members of Roosevelt's administration who opposed his
ideas. In particular, Hull was locked in combat with George
N. Peek, the president's adviser on foreign trade. Roosevelt
accepted Hull's trade policies, but, paradoxically, the president appointed Peek, an economic nationalist, to the newly
created interdepartmental Executive Committee on Commercial Policy.[43] The secretary and State Department officials opposed the appointment because Peek favored a trade
barrier to imports while the domestic recovery programs
were applied. If Peek succeeded, the trade agreements were
doomed.

Some State Department policy makers comforted themselves in the belief that Roosevelt was easing Peek out of the
administration by giving him responsibilities in foreign

trade.[44] They underestimated Peek. Soon after his appointment to the committee, Peek submitted his own report to the president recommending that he be made chairman. Assistant Secretary Francis Sayre headed the committee, so if the change were implemented it would rob the State Department of control over foreign trade. A second recommendation in the report proposed a new agency to regulate trade, with Peek as director.[45]

The State Department lost its first battle with Peek. The report found its way into the press, and the publicity forced the president to make a hasty decision, naming Peek chairman of the Executive Committee on Commercial Policy. When the State Department discovered that Peek had succeeded, sentiment was divided between those who urged Hull to appeal to the president to reverse the decision and those who believed that Peek's ambition would soon outrun his ability.[46]

Peek and the State Department clashed over the Trade Agreements Act passed in June 1934. Hull, elated by congressional endorsement, assumed that the State Department would retain control.[47] The assumption proved false, for one part of the act established a subcommittee to the Executive Committee on Commercial Policy with large power to negotiate over foreign trade. The secretary of state expected to appoint the chairman from the State Department, but when suggestions along these lines were presented to the Executive Committee all agreed except Peek. To the State Department's despair, Peek still enjoyed presidential favor. With the aid of several subordinates Hull drew up a new proposal omitting reference to the secretary's right to appoint a chairman and recommending that subcommittee members elect their chairman. The alternative circumvented Peek's objection, for it was taken for granted that the subcommittee would choose a department official as chairman.

Further difficulties with Peek materialized in the autumn of 1934. The president continued to defend Peek and even advised Hull to cooperate with his adversary. He wrote Hull,

"I am inclined to think that if you and George Peek who represents the very hard-headed practical angle of trade, could spend a couple of hours some evening together talking over this problem of the most-favored-nation clauses, it would be helpful in many ways."[48]

Roosevelt failed to understand the bitterness between the two men and the State Department's exasperation when dealing with Peek. The president did not at first recognize Peek's desire to destroy the Hull Program but became aware of it when Peek attacked the department blatantly. On November 20, Peek delivered a speech charging that the failure of the United States to sell in foreign markets was the fault of "a school of international altruists" who believed in free trade. He recommended that the government change its policy and instead assist exports, subsidizing them if necessary; adopt a two-price system for stipulated commodities, one for the United States and one for foreign trade; change the unconditional most-favored-nation policy to selective importation and export; and adopt two-column tariff and import quotas granting preferential treatment to goods from countries providing better outlets for American goods. If adopted, these proposals would destroy Hull's program. The secretary retaliated by publicly attacking Peek and reaffirming the department's intention to retain unconditional most-favored-nation treatment.[49]

Although problems with Peek continued into 1935, the fight ended. The department won. The president lost faith in Peek and on one occasion showed Undersecretary Phillips a letter from him that amounted to resignation. Moreover, Peek's loss of influence was evident in his behavior. No longer in a position to demand, he pleaded for changes in the trade program.[50]

What did the department win for itself and the country? Although Hull managed to conclude eighteen treaties under authority of the Trade Agreements Act of 1934, the gains were negligible. The United States remained a creditor nation, and Roosevelt never decided whether to use the system to promote world trade or as a ruse to enlarge foreign markets.[51] The trade program did nothing to eliminate international economic problems or restore domestic prosperity.

Hull believed his reciprocal trade program would promote political reciprocity. He saw in the give-and-take on economic issues a basis for restoration of political comity. But the political consequences of the program were only slightly more consequential than the economic. There is evidence that although economic cooperation was modest, some accomplishments occurred. In the case of Britain, for example, although a trade agreement was slow in coming and inconsequential economically, it promoted some sort of harmony.[52] But the trade agreements failed to promote cooperation with the expansionist states or those opposing the expansion of Germany, Italy, and Japan.

Ultimately the blame for failure of the Trade Agreements Act to achieve its lofty purposes must be placed on Hull. Hull's "ruminative" mind led him to a repetition of the formula that lower trade barriers equal peace. Other nations refused to accept his solution. His approach rested on a false analogy. He assumed that nations would behave like members of Congress, bargaining vigorously and trading actively, and from that atmosphere of give-and-take would ensue peace and prosperity. But world trade and world politics did not prove to be subject to the same rules as congressional behavior.

Liberalization of trade as a limited economic objective had some merit. But Hull overextended his freer trade principle, making it a universal formula. In short, Hull failed to define an economic program that was carefully tailored to meet the demands of the depression at home and abroad.

2. Recognition of the Soviet Union

Hull was not alone in the search for a golden key to unlock the treasures of economic internationalism and thereby end the depression. The president and others saw an equally lucrative answer in the establishment of diplomatic relations with the Soviet Union as a way to increase trade. Senators William E. Borah of Idaho and Hiram W. Johnson of California believed that nonrecognition had unfortunate economic consequences in light of the depressed condition of the United States. Business leaders shared this view. James D. Mooney, vice-president of General Motors, told the American Automobile Club of Paris that diplomatic relations were essential if the United States hoped to realize the commercial opportunities in Russia. While Roosevelt may not have shared this view, he sought to end the anomalous situation. Possibly he sensed the need to find a counterweight to the threat of German and Japanese expansion.[1]

Like other issues, recognition of the Soviet Union was a carry-over from an earlier period. The United States was antagonistic to the Soviet Union from the outset of the Bolshevik takeover. Wilson had little sympathy for godless radicals who abandoned their allies at a crucial time, and he refused to extend recognition. That decision represented a departure from a longstanding tradition, initiated when Thomas Jefferson was secretary of state, of extending recognition promptly to de facto governments no matter what forms these governments might take. The tradition had prevailed for over a century when Wilson reversed it.

Others saw the Bolshevik triumph differently. William C. Bullitt, a young aristocrat in the State Department who was later to figure prominently in the recognition negotiations, worked in the West European Division of the department under a young career officer, Joseph Grew, and Undersecretary Phillips. Here among other young blue bloods, Bullitt displayed restless idealism and brash self-confidence. The Russian Revolution symbolized to him and many others an event of profound meaning. He saw it as a great spiritual awakening.[2]

Bullitt's wealth, position, and keen intelligence contributed to an assertiveness that bordered on arrogance. Although his position in the State Department was modest, it did not stop him from acquainting his superiors with the soundness of his advice. In January 1918, he made it a practice to write unsolicited memorandums to Colonel House, Wilson's adviser, Phillips, and even the president. At that early date, when Russia was looking toward withdrawal from the war, he was advocating the advantages to be gained from extending recognition to the Bolsheviks.[3] He was ignored, but only for the moment.

Gradually, Bullitt's advice began to have an effect. He cultivated a friendship with House and took advantage of the relationship to persuade House to arrange to have him included in the peace delegation to Paris. Bullitt's good fortune continued at the conference. Wilson needed someone to investigate conditions in Russia. Wilson and the British prime minister, David Lloyd George, felt it necessary to make a decision about the withdrawal of Allied troops engaged in an intervention in Siberia and North Russia. Because little was known about conditions in Russia, House recommended a secret investigation headed by Bullitt. Bullitt apparently was impressed with the effectiveness of Bolshevik control and was convinced that Russia would become socialist. He drafted terms for a peace agreement between Russia and the Allies, but Wilson and the other negotiators at Paris rejected the proposal. Bullitt's disappointment over the rejection and his extreme dissatisfaction with the Versailles Treaty prompted him to resign from the delegation in May 1919 and to become an opponent of Wilson.[4]

During the senatorial debate on the treaty, Bullitt earned for himself the title of traitor among his Democratic colleagues. As Senator Henry Cabot Lodge's star witness, Bullitt gave testimony that contributed to the downfall of the treaty. As a result, he was ostracized politically. It was years before he made a comeback, and even then his "turncoat" reputation plagued him. Bullitt's political and personal image was that of "an emotional, erratic, not entirely trustworthy man—a person who 'talked too much.' "[5] Despite these handicaps, he would help Roosevelt decide to recognize the Soviet Union.

Commerce brought the United States and the Soviet Union together without formal diplomatic ties. Following the war, trade between the Soviet Union and the United States increased rapidly.[6] Most of the trade was channeled through Amtorg, the Soviet trading company, incorporated in New York. Amtorg purchased goods from Russian producers for resale in the United States and represented Russian firms placing orders in America. Amtorg grew to the point that by 1929 most Soviet commerce flowed through it. Later this corporation was involved in the first steps toward recognition.

The year 1929 was a turning point in relations between the United States and the Soviet Union. Increasing exports to the Soviet Union in 1929 and 1930 prompted some leading American businessmen to advocate recognition. Curiously, in the period 1929 to 1933 economic considerations worked in opposite ways in the two countries. At the outset the Russians were interested primarily in economic ties and secondarily in political ties, whereas the United States was not interested in the Soviet market until 1932 when the depression deepened. Then Soviet economic concerns declined and political considerations became more important as the Far Eastern situation grew more ominous for Russia.[7]

Hoover opposed recognition. His secretary of state, Stimson, favored recognition, but department officials hesitated to establish diplomatic relations.[8] Indicative of the official view was Undersecretary of State William R. Castle's letter to a New Jersey industrialist who favored establishing commercial relations with Russia. Castle pointed to the lack of good faith the Russians had shown and said he doubted that recognition of the Soviet Union would lead to a substantial increase in its purchases in the United States. He concluded with the observation that "the establishment of relations with Russia under present conditions would not appreciably alter the attitude of your banking connections with respect to Russian trade acceptances."[9] Apparently the department, reflecting the official position of the Hoover administration, could see no economic imperatives for recognition.

The new administration thought differently; Roosevelt was determined to recognize the Soviet Union. Other nations had established relations with the regime, and he thought it anomalous for the United States to continue nonrecognition. Roosevelt was less moved by economic considerations than were many advocates of recognition. For him, political considerations were paramount. Feis recalls that "The idea was forming in both Roosevelt's and Hull's minds that Japan and Germany might be sobered if the breach between the United States and the Soviet Union were healed."[10] Roosevelt recognized the absurdity of denying recognition when many other major powers had extended it.[11]

But Roosevelt did not embark on the recognition quest alone. Close at hand were two advisers who participated in the discussion leading to recognition, Bullitt and Henry Morgenthau, Jr.

After a prolonged sojourn in the wilderness following his falling-out with his party, Bullitt wanted to reenter public life. He was so affected by Roosevelt's campaign that he wrote to Colonel House asking for his help in joining the Roosevelt cause. Years before, House had been impressed with Bullitt's intelligence, so he promised to help, but the extent of his influence was questionable. In July 1932, Bullitt contacted Louis B. Wehle, a classmate of FDR and a successful New York lawyer. In August, Wehle wrote to

Roosevelt extolling Bullitt's value because of his recent con-
tacts with the leading statesmen of Europe, adding that Bullitt would be valuable in the campaign on matters relating
to foreign affairs. At first Roosevelt was not disposed to bring
Bullitt into his group of advisers. But after the November
1932 election, during a discussion on the debt issue with
FDR, Wehle suggested that Bullitt be asked to go on a fact-
finding mission to Europe. Bullitt, Wehle pointed out, could
use his own resources and learn what European cabinets
were likely to do about debt installments due in December.
FDR saw no harm in the scheme and thereby started his
practice of using personal emissaries abroad. The fact that
FDR did not mention the trip or its purpose to Moley, who
was already studying the debt situation, anticipated a presidential practice of never letting his right-hand man know
what his left-hand man was doing.[12] Bullitt sent back information to the president-elect about the attitudes of leading
European officials, particularly Prime Minister Ramsey J.
MacDonald of Britain and Premier Edouard Herriot of
France.

But Bullitt compromised his position when he revealed
the purpose of his trip to a friend and newspaper stories
brought his mission to light. His old reputation of talking too
much came back to haunt him. Although the incident blew
over without serious repercussions for Bullitt or the administration, it put into question whether he should be used in
an official capacity in the new administration. In the end
Moley brought Bullitt into the government. Moley kept reminding Roosevelt about Bullitt's interest, but the president
seemed hesitant. Perhaps he was influenced by Phillips, who
reminded FDR that Bullitt had been a traitor to the Wilson
administration.[13] Phillips finally gave in, however, and suggested that Bullitt be given the position of special assistant
to the secretary of state rather than assistant secretary. The
latter post would involve senatorial approval and might
open old sores. Roosevelt agreed. Bullitt was back in government. It is possible that FDR's reason for reclaiming Bullitt
was his intention to recognize the Soviet Union. In any case
Bullitt became the president's closest aide on recognition.

Morgenthau was the other adviser who helped initiate recognition discussions. Soon after Roosevelt took office, the Farm Credit Board, the Reconstruction Finance Corporation, and the Treasury Department considered the prospects of financing sales of farm products and manufactured goods to Russia with various business groups. Nothing came of these discussions, and Roosevelt said to Morgenthau in May 1933, "Gosh, if I could only myself talk to some one man representing the Russians, I could straighten out the whole question. If you get the opportunity, Henry, you could say that you believe, but have no authority to say so, that the President would like to send some person to Moscow as Trade Commissioner in order to break the ice between the two countries and in that way gradually get people of the United States used to doing business with the Russians." Morgenthau interpreted this statement to mean that Roosevelt felt there was opposition to his plans in the State Department.[14]

Some members of the department were skeptical about sudden moves toward recognition and advised caution. Among them was the chief of the East European Division, Robert F. Kelley, who, on July 27, 1933, submitted a memorandum which formed the basis of the department's position. Kelley asserted that there were serious obstacles in the path of recognition that had to be removed to prevent future friction. He listed the obstacles: the world revolutionary aims of the Soviet Union; its unwillingness to respect the rights of citizens of other states; its failure to honor the financial obligations of preceding governments; its monopoly over foreign trade, which placed individual business concerns there at a disadvantage; and its alien conception of justice, which included an excessively broad definition of economic espionage.[15]

The ideas expressed in this memorandum were echoed by others in the State Department. Caution was the common advice of all those involved in the recognition deliberations. On September 21, 1933, for example, Hull sent a memorandum to FDR which, in essence, repeated the argument advanced by Kelley. Hull enumerated the same obstacles

Kelley had and went on to say that the Soviet Union wanted two things from the United States—credits and recognition. Russia was having difficulty meeting its financial obligations to Germany and could benefit from American help. On the political front, the Russians feared the growing ambition of Japan in the Maritime Provinces and wanted recognition. Thus, Hull reasoned, the United States had two powerful weapons to use in bringing about a favorable resolution to outstanding problems with the Soviets. The United States could withhold support in both areas of interest to the Soviets until American claims were satisfied.[16]

On September 26, a few days after Roosevelt received the forceful views of the State Department, he met with Morgenthau, who by that time was handling all financing of exports to Russia. Morgenthau asked Roosevelt if he wanted to make loans to Russia "in view of the publicity now surrounding that prospect." Roosevelt dodged the issue, asking, "What would you think of bringing this whole Russian question into our front parlor instead of back in the kitchen? . . . I have a plan in mind." Although he did not explain what he meant, he suggested that Morgenthau send for Boris Skivsky, the director of the Soviet Information Bureau in Washington, and intimate to Skivsky that the American government was considering the question of recognition, not only the extension of credits. The following day, September 27, Morgenthau and Bullitt lunched together and discussed the Russian matter. Up to this time, Bullitt had worked on the problem of recognition in a general way, following, in essence, the policy advocated by Kelley and others. Bullitt's interest quickened when he saw the president was moving more quickly in the direction of recognition. Morgenthau recalls that "Bullitt began walking me to work in the mornings in order to pump me about the latest developments. At first this annoyed the President, on the ground that Bullitt was going over Hull's head. . . . But, as affairs developed, he entrusted the negotiations more and more to Bullitt."[17]

Once again, as in the case of the London economic conference, Roosevelt circumvented the lines of command in the department. Roosevelt realized that the department either opposed recognition or was very cautious. He had reason to doubt its enthusiasm. Phillips, the new undersecretary, remembered, "Some of us in the Department, including myself, regretted Roosevelt's action, which automatically put us on the defensive, whereas it could easily have been arranged for Russia to make the first move. We realized that there would be severe criticism if the terms of recognition were not satisfactory from the American point of view."[18] Others shared Phillips's reserve. Robert F. Kelley was skeptical because he believed that the revolutionary aims and practices of the Soviet Union would prevent amiable relations with other states.

Yet, although Kelley would have been satisfied to continue the nonrecognition policy, he later limited his concern to how the United States might best protect its interests once it was decided to extend recognition.[19] Kelley's reaction indicates a difference between the two instances of Roosevelt's circumvention of the Department. Unlike the London conference the recognition question involved no difference of opinion between Secretary Hull and a special presidential assistant or others. On October 4, for example, Hull received memorandums from Bullitt and from Assistant Secretary of State R. Walton Moore. Moore argued that although recognition should not be delayed, there must be assurance that the Russians would not directly or indirectly "affect the political institutions or integrity of the United States and that certain other major matters can be satisfactorily disposed of." He also pointed out that "Russia was more reasonable toward nations that had not granted recognition than those that have and after recognition became indifferent to her obligations."[20] Bullitt made similar observations. Like Moore and others, he argued that recognition and loans should be withheld until agreement was reached on a number of outstanding questions. Bullitt listed three issues that had to be agreed upon before recognition: a prohibition against communist propaganda in the United States, protection of civil and religious rights of Americans in Russia, and recognition to take effect only from the day on which it was accorded.[21] Thus in the department there was a broad base of procedural agreement before the initial invitation to the Russians to embark upon recognition negotiations.[22]

The next step toward recognition involved an informal meeting with Skivsky. Morgenthau helped to bring him and Bullitt together. On October 11, 1933, Bullitt and Morgenthau met with Skivsky and presented him with a letter that had already been seen and approved by Roosevelt and Hull.[23] Bullitt said, "I have a piece of paper in my hand. It is unsigned. It can be made into an invitation for you to send representatives here to discuss diplomatic relations. We wish you to telegraph it by your most confidential code and learn if it is acceptable. . . . If not, will you give me your word of honor that there never will be any publicity about this proposed exchange of letters and that the whole matter will be kept secret?"[24] Skivsky agreed to the terms and asked Bullitt if that meant recognition. Bullitt answered: "What more can you expect than to have your representative sit down with the President of the United States?"[25]

Roosevelt's invitation to President Mikhall Kalinin to discuss normal relations was answered promptly. Soviet Commissar Maxim Litvinov would be sent to Washington to represent the Soviet Union in the discussions. The exchange of letters was released to the press. Almost immediately expressions of concern were heard from department officials, particularly those associated with Far Eastern developments. Hornbeck wrote to Hull on October 28: "It is believed that consideration should be given to ways and means, if possible, of reassuring the Japanese, that is of definitely combating the growth of any impression that the forthcoming conversations between American and Russian representatives are in part motivated by and will in part relate to problems in the Far East which have arisen in consequence of Japanese policy and action."[26]

On November 6, the day before Litvinov arrived, Roosevelt met with Hull, Phillips, Bullitt, Morgenthau, and Moore. They agreed, according to Hull, that the "two most important precautions were against Soviet propaganda and illegal activities in the United States and freedom of worship for Americans in Russia."[27] Two days later, when the secretary, along with Phillips, Moore, Bullitt, Kelley, and Morgenthau, met with Litvinov these issues and others were included. The department officials outlined the United States position on propaganda, religious rights, legal prerogatives, and repayments of loans to the Kerensky provisional government.

Although the exchange was friendly, it was apparent that Litvinov was not authorized to grant the American government any concessions on these matters. Litvinov dodged each issue. He argued that Americans in the USSR were allowed religious freedom, recommended that payment of American loans and claims be dealt with after recognition, and disclaimed all responsibility for the activities of the Third Communist International in the United States. The fruitless exchange on November 8 and 9 led to an impasse.[28] Roosevelt spoke to Litvinov the next day. The president exercised his famous charm and in a remarkable display of personal diplomacy convinced Litvinov to reconsider his position on at least one issue, Soviet propaganda in the United States. Resolution of this matter finally came when Bullitt intervened and handed Litvinov a document of agreement on propaganda along with a schedule of ship sailings. The message was clear, and Litvinov relented.[29]

The religious question was raised as well, this time forcefully. On November 11, Litvinov agreed to a statement on religious freedom that would satisfy the president. Litvinov did not agree to the legal issue involving Americans who were imprisoned in the Soviet Union. For five more days, from November 12 to 16, negotiations continued. Finally on the evening of the sixteenth, after a social event at the White House, Roosevelt read Litvinov the text of letters of understanding between the two governments leading to recognition. The letters were signed, and by this act diplomatic relations were opened.

The letter extending recognition was followed by other letters outlining mutual understandings. Among the more significant was a Soviet guarantee not to interfere in the internal affairs of the United States. Another involved the exercise of religious freedom by Americans in Russia. The third was a Soviet promise to grant American nationals the same legal protection enjoyed by nationals of any foreign country. And, fourth, the Soviets relinquished any claims against America as a result of the 1919 American military actions in Siberia. Roosevelt and Litvinov also announced their agreement on repayment of American loans to the Kerensky regime. The Soviets agreed to pay not less than $75 million in the form of a percentage above the usual rate of interest on a loan to be granted by the United States or its nationals.

These understandings caused no particular concern to the State Department, and the "gentlemen's agreement" on Russian debts, though unpublished at that time, was a secondary matter to Bullitt and other State Department officials. Morgenthau wrote, "I don't think that Bullitt and some of the others were much interested in the financial aspect of recognition." Moore announced in a radio address following the recognition announcement that the debt settlement was "altogether ancillary."[30]

Recognition of the Soviet Union without undue public rancor was a diplomatic triumph for the Roosevelt administration and an example of direct intervention by the president. Roosevelt ignored the department's hierarchy and enlisted the support of Bullitt, a subordinate to those State Department officials who had expressed strong reservations about recognition. Division Chief Kelley and Undersecretary Phillips did not share Bullitt's enthusiasm, but they finally accepted the idea of recognition provided that concessions were exacted before recognition was granted. In short, the differences that existed between Roosevelt, Bullitt, and Morgenthau, on the one hand, and Phillips, Kelley, and Hull, on the other, were ones of degree or method rather than substance. Roosevelt believed recognition was necessary in order to give the United States a listening post in Russia. To achieve that end, FDR was willing to move more boldly than were some department skeptics.

As a diplomatic team, Roosevelt and Bullitt were perfectly matched. When negotiations reached an impasse, Bullitt played the heavy while Roosevelt smoothed things over. As a result, between them they achieved agreements with the Soviets that were the broadest ever concluded.[31] Russia agreed to grant religious freedom and legal protection to Americans in the Soviet Union, to refrain from propagandizing in the United States, to revise its definition of espionage (excluding economic activities), and to waive claims growing out of American interest in the country in 1918. Admittedly, some of the agreed-upon points such as the "gentlemen's agreement" and the promise on communist propagandizing were soon forgotten. But it is doubtful that any other approach, including the more cautious diplomacy advocated by career department officials and by Hull, would have worked better.

Roosevelt's success, however, was lessened somewhat by his treatment of Hull. By ignoring Hull in favor of personal emissaries both within and without the department, Roosevelt diluted Hull's authority in foreign affairs. Although Hull did not register the same concern over Bullitt's behavior as he had over Moley's at the London economic conference, he was sensitive about his diminishing position.[32]

With recognition accomplished, it was a foregone conclusion that Bullitt would be the first ambassador. Roosevelt had decided in December 1932 to select Bullitt if recognition became a reality, and he reaffirmed that decision before Hull left for the Montevideo conference. If Roosevelt had any doubts about the choice, they were dispelled after the signing of the recognition agreements on November 16, 1933. At the time, Roosevelt asked Phillips for his opinion of Bullitt. Phillips reversed his earlier judgment and praised Bullitt.[33] Roosevelt then appointed Bullitt.

Although Bullitt was the obvious choice, in many ways he was a liability. His idealism combined with a deep need to be liked made him vulnerable to flattery and disillusionment. Moreover, his long exile had intensified his need to feel that he was an insider at the White House and at the

Kremlin.[34] In a personal letter to Roosevelt, dated January 1, 1934, one of many he was to write from abroad, Bullitt relates how warmly he was received in Moscow. On December 20, nine days after his arrival, he was invited to a dinner given by Supreme Commander Kliment Varoshilov of the Soviet army and navy. After many toasts, Bullitt felt himself an insider. He related that "everyone at the table got into the mood of a college fraternity banquet, and discretion was conspicuous by its absence. Litvinov whispered to me, 'You told me that you wouldn't stay here if you were going to be treated as an outsider. Do you realize that everyone at this table has completely forgotten that anyone is here except the members of this inner gang?' That certainly seemed to be the case."[35] The hosts quickly sensed Bullitt's need to be liked and used it to their advantage.

The Soviet officials wanted Bullitt to help them enlist American support against Japan. At that same dinner, Bullitt received a clear impression that "the Soviet Government values so highly the moral support it may receive from the United States in the matter of preventing war with Japan that there is almost nothing we may not ask for and obtain at the present time." Actually, as Stalin had indicated at that dinner, the Russians had more than moral support in mind. Stalin wanted steel rails from the United States to complete the Soviet railroad to Vladivostok.[36] More important, the Soviets wanted a bilateral nonaggression pact with the United States. Litvinov had made such a proposal in November but was turned down by Roosevelt. Here the president was following the lead of Undersecretary Phillips, who showed no enthusiasm.[37]

The Russians may have hoped that Bullitt could reverse the administration's resistance to their proposals. But as events developed, they could not use him or anyone else to alter the American position on the Far East. As early as 1934, diverse misapprehensions created a mutually disappointing relationship between Bullitt and the Russians. The Soviets failed to use Bullitt effectively to change American policy. He was no longer made to feel he was part of the inner circle, and he reacted vehemently.

During the first half of 1934, Bullitt and his Soviet hosts were cordial with one another, though some signs of stress were already evident. In March 1934, Bullitt informed the State Department of three misunderstandings. Two were relatively minor: the Soviet government did not provide rubles for embassy use, and the property Stalin promised for the American embassy was not available. A third was serious. It involved Litvinov's interpretation of the "gentlemen's agreement." Apparently, Litvinov, in his initial discussions with Bullitt about debts, argued that he had agreed to payment of Soviet obligations in return for a straight loan of $100 million which could be used anywhere, as opposed to a commercial credit in the United States.[38]

Bullitt and Litvinov were at odds over the "gentlemen's agreement." Litvinov, for example, rejected the Department of State's draft proposal which set the amount of indebtedness at $150 million with an interest rate of 5 percent. The debt would be retired by an additional interest payment of 10 percent on all credits or loans extended to the Soviet government or its nationals. The additional interest would go first toward the interest accruing on the $100 million and thereafter toward the reduction of the principal. Although the proposal represented maximum demands and was open to negotiation, Litvinov refused to bargain. Again he returned to the promise of a loan to the USSR.[39]

The Bullitt-Litvinov negotiations took on a new and different meaning when Congress passed the Johnson Act on April 4, 1934. It forbade loans to governments in default to the United States. Litvinov came up with a counterproposal on May 9, but after he departed for Geneva it was apparent that there was no real change in the Soviet position. When Litvinov returned from Geneva, he accused the United States of trying to back out of its agreement. The argument continued without resolution. Finally, Litvinov said the matter should be dropped because no government pays it debts.[40]

Commissar Litvinov's argument was not completely unfounded. Litvinov's memorandum of May 9 had mentioned a loan. Roosevelt and Bullitt, moreover, carelessly had said "loan" but meant "credit." Litvinov's position is further strengthened by the fact that Assistant Secretary Moore in a memorandum to Assistant Secretary Sayre implied that control of credits, an American assumption, was not made explicit until the Moscow talks on debts. There is written documentation to support Litvinov's claim about the promise of a loan, as State Department experts admitted in a November 15, 1945, interdepartment memorandum. In this instance, Bullitt and Roosevelt revealed their lack of knowledge of diplomatic procedure by assuming that Litvinov knew what they meant and would follow their unwritten intentions.[41]

Acrimonious debate between Litvinov and Bullitt continued into the autumn of 1934. But the argument did not immediately alter Bullitt's friendly feelings toward the Soviet Union. Rather, it gave him a chance to ventilate his anger against the Soviets. Bullitt continued to court, and he courted in Russia. He hoped to counteract Litvinov's influence by cultivating friends in the military. To this end he tried to teach the Red Army cavalry to play polo, introduced baseball, and threw the best party in Moscow.[42]

These efforts failed. By the middle of 1935, Bullitt did an about-face, abandoning his friendly feelings for Russia. The event that precipitated Bullitt's abrupt change of heart was the convocation of the Comintern in Moscow in July 1935.[43] The meeting was held under the auspices of the Soviet government, which made available one of the largest government buildings in the city and placed the press and Tass agency at the disposal of the congress. More important, representatives of the American Communist party were present and figured prominently in the proceedings. By allowing American communist participation in the congress the Russians violated their pledge of November 1933 "not to permit the formation or residence on its territory of any organization or group . . . which has as an aim the overthrow or the preparation for the overthrow of, or the bringing about by force of a change in the political or social order of the whole or any part of the United States."[44]

In July, Bullitt wrote to Roosevelt expressing his deep

concern over the Comintern and speculating on how the United States might respond to the Soviets' violations of their pledge:

> If the violation should be merely technical and if you should feel that we cannot ignore it, I think we should confine our action to an oral protest by me to Litvinov, a simultaneous withdrawal of the exequatius [authorization of a consul by a foreign government] of the Soviet Consuls in New York and San Francisco and a tightening of our liberal policy of giving visas to the United States to Soviet officials.

On the other hand, Bullitt continued, "If the violation should be not technical but gross and insulting, I suspect that you will feel obliged to break relations."[45]

Finally, he conjectured that "if the violation should fall between the two extremes and be neither technical nor gross and insulting (and I think it will fall between the extremes) it will be most difficult to decide what to do." But he hoped that it would all blow over and that relations would continue because it seemed likely that the USSR would become involved in war in both the Far East and Europe in the near future. Consequently, it was wise to continue diplomatic relations.[46] In any event, Bullitt cautioned, "I think we should avoid at all costs the usual practice of writing a large pontifical note of protest."[47] Yet this is what Roosevelt and Hull did. The following month they instructed Bullitt to deliver a note to the Soviet foreign office protesting Russian violation of the pledge to discourage American communists.

The Comintern represented a significant turning point in Bullitt's attitude. He was too emotional to accept the Russian violation. After the meeting Bullitt recalled, "I deviled the Russians. I did all I could to make things unpleasant."[48] His behavior became unacceptable for a diplomat. He urged, for example, American and foreign newspaper correspondents to take an anti-Soviet stance. By 1936 Bullitt was a liability in Moscow. Consequently, a June leave of absence became a permanent leave. In August he was appointed ambassador to France.

When Bullitt left the Soviet Union, the first phase of American relations with that country came to an end. During the initial period, from the recognition negotiations until the ambassador was reassigned, Bullitt was a major influence on foreign policy. His most significant role was that of a negotiator at the time of recognition. Later, as the diplomatic representative in Moscow, he and his subordinates in the embassy found his first diplomatic tour very satisfying. But his tour ended in deep frustration because the Soviets reneged on three promises which he regarded as a *quid pro quo* for recognition: stopping subversive propaganda in the United States; permitting the building of an embassy on the Sparrow Hills overlooking the Moscow River; and making arrangements for currency exchange that would allow the American embassy to function properly. In the autumn of 1933 when the Russians made these promises, they feared Japanese aggression. After mid-1934 when that threat abated, the Soviets were less cooperative. According to one of his former subordinates, George F. Kennan, Bullitt "had done his job in Moscow, with verve and enthusiasm; and he was conscious of having done it well. It was not his fault if he had been deceived." The experience left Bullitt so embittered that his views of Russia were no longer regarded as trustworthy. But Bullitt offered sound advice before he left the post on April 20, 1936. He cautioned that "we should neither expect too much nor despair of getting anything at all."[49] If the State Department had followed this advice in its dealings with the Soviet Union, American interests might have been considerably advanced. Regrettably, many expected too much from the Soviets and consequently despaired too greatly when those expectations went unfulfilled.

Indeed, the recognition issue reveals that the State Department expected more than it should have from that diplomatic tool. For example, Stanley K. Hornbeck, head of the Far Eastern Division, concerned with the political implications of recognition of the Soviet Union in power relationships in the Far East, even suggested at one point that recognition might be used to gain concessions from the Soviets in the Far East. Presumably he was thinking of preventing greater Soviet influence on China. As events unfolded, in the Far East and elsewhere, United States recognition of the Soviet Union had no influence on world politics.[50]

3. Recognizing Others: Cuba and Liberia

Recognition of the Soviet government was a routine occurrence in that it had no immediate profound effect on the course of events. In other instances during the early New Deal period, the granting or withholding of recognition had immediate and sometimes devastating effects. Small and weak countries that were dependent upon American economic ties, especially countries in which the economy was based primarily upon a single extractive industry, could not afford action that might upset trade. The potent effects of a nonrecognition policy to promote American interests were clearly demonstrated in relations with Cuba and Liberia.

American foreign policy with respect to Cuba during Roosevelt's first administration continued a pattern of close connection between investment, trade, and Cuban stability developed from 1898 to 1919. United States influence guaranteed protection of investments in Cuba, expansion of trade with the island, and Cuban tranquility. From 1919 to 1933, the financial commitment in Central and South America grew because American businessmen and government officials believed that the Latin American market was vital to the economy of the country. Cuba became a pivotal area in economic relations with the Latin American states as a result of the growing belief that American actions there directly influenced U.S. trade with other Latin American countries.[1]

The State Department worked closely with American business interests in Cuba. Although some disagreements

over specific tactics emerged in the 1898-1919 period, general accord existed regarding basic goals. From 1919 to 1933,
department officials and businessmen concurred on motives
and methods in relations with Cuba. Both wanted stability
to ensure the protection of economic interests. Democratic
reforms in Cuba were supported by the United States when
such concessions seemed necessary to quiet potential trou-
blemakers. From 1923 to 1931, the situation in Cuba was
peaceful enough for the United States to avoid encouraging
reform.[2] Maintaining the status quo represented the cardinal principle of America's Cuban policy.

From 1925 to 1933, Cuba was dominated by a business-
man who actively supported American interests. The Cuban
president in this period, Gerardo Machado, was viewed as
the personification of stability by Americans until the Great
Depression. Economic dislocation and Machado's repressive
domestic program made him a liability to the United States,
but even though the State Department was aware of the
growing opposition to Machado, it continued to support his
regime. Undoubtedly, the department's attitude was condi-
tioned by the continued support of the Machado regime by
American business interests. Moreover, from 1928 to 1932
both President Hoover and Secretary of State Stimson were
anxious to change America's image in the Western Hemisphere. In the past, direct intervention had had an adverse
effect on United States commercial expansion in Latin
America. With this historical lesson in mind, Stimson
pointed out that accusations of American imperialism "have
damaged our good name, our credit, and our trade far
beyond the apprehension of our people."[3] Hence, the Hoover
administration planned to withdraw Marines from Haiti
and Nicaragua and maintain a hands-off policy in Cuba.
Hands-off meant supporting Machado, who represented the
status quo.

At the beginning of Roosevelt's first administration, important business groups were clamoring for measures to increase exports. Reviving the Cuban market, often cited as
one of the most urgent problems confronting the administra-

tion, was regarded by American businessmen as a testing ground for the Good Neighbor policy.[4] Thus, relations with Cuba emerged as a singularly important issue in the early New Deal period.

The chief architect of State Department policy with respect to Cuba was the ambassador, Sumner Welles, a career diplomat with experience in Latin American policy. He believed that the role of the United States in the Western Hemisphere, especially in the Caribbean, should be one of "friendly intervention," a policy designed to obtain stable and cooperative governments sympathetic to the wishes of the United States. Although some members of the department had misgivings about his approach, Welles's interventionist tactic was adopted, for the important voices in the State Department approved of his objective—the creation of a situation in Cuba conducive to American expansion.[5]

At first, the department treated Cuba with forbearance. Ambassador Welles discussed Cuban difficulties with President Machado, assuring him that the United States did not interpret its obligations under the Platt Amendment as a license to meddle in Cuba's domestic affairs. That amendment to the army appropriation bill of 1901 had made Cuba a protectorate of the United States, and its restrictive provisions had been incorporated in a treaty between the two countries in 1903. Among the more significant features of the amendment was the right of the United States to intervene in Cuba to preserve order. Welles emphasized the necessity for promoting order in the country and promised American aid to that end. Once stability prevailed in Cuba, the United States could enter into a reciprocal trade agreement with the island nation. Such an agreement, the ambassador hinted, would materially aid Machado's cause by distracting the Cuban people from political agitation.[6]

Welles informed the department of his meeting with Machado and urged the department to negotiate a commercial agreement with Cuba for two reasons: the United States had lost ground in the Cuban market in the preceding ten years and needed to recoup those commercial losses; and an economic agreement with Cuba would distract the Cuban people and prevent social unrest. The State Department endorsed Welles's recommendations and instructed him to proceed with trade negotiations.[7]

Several months after Welles's talk with President Machado, the ambassador, with department consent, embarked upon a program of direct interference in Cuban domestic affairs. When revolutionary agitation reached a critical point in the summer of 1933, Welles on his own initiative acted as mediator between various opposition groups.[8] Not satisfied with an unofficial role, the ambassador requested departmental instructions to inform Machado that if the Cuban leader refused American, that is, Welles's mediation, the United States would withdraw recognition of the Cuban government.[9] The department concurred, thereby officially sanctioning the ambassador's interventionist diplomacy. But Welles was not satisfied simply to mediate in Cuba. He notified Machado that he should resign because of the opposition to his regime.[10] Shortly thereafter, Machado was overthrown by the Cuban army with Welles's blessings.

Initially Welles and the State Department supported Machado's successor, Grau San Martin. The ambassador disregarded reports about radical elements in the new Cuban government as fantasies of American business interests. The "Sergeant's Revolt" of September 5, 1933, when Sergeant Fulgencio Batista took control of the army and later the government, however, convinced Welles that the stories about radicalization were true, and he requested American military assistance. At least twenty-nine naval vessels were ordered to Cuba, Marine air squadrons were alerted, and pilots at Quantico, Virginia, were mobilized.[11] Military preparations of that extent meant intimidation, not protection. Welles even suggested that a small number of American Marines "assist" the Cuban government in maintaining order, though the ambassador did not favor a prolonged intervention by troops.[12]

Some members of the department disapproved of the interventionist tactics in Cuba. Josephus Daniels, the Ameri-

can ambassador to Mexico, believed the tales of com-
munist-inspired attacks on American property were exaggerated, and he advised Hull to "accept with many grains
of allowance the attempt to blame on the comparatively few
Communists all that goes awry."[13] He decried the use of
military force in Cuba, noting that Cuban unrest was a result of "American owners of sugar plantations and mines
and other property who do not pay living wages to Cuban
workers. They wish American troops to protect them in paying such miserable wages."[14] Other members of the department shared Daniels's dissatisfaction with American policy
in Cuba. Undersecretary Phillips wrote in his diary, "Welles
is doing no good in Havana; he has become so involved with
the various political parties and is being so violently attacked in the local press and otherwise that his presence
there has no longer any 'healing' effect."[15] But the dissenters
were ignored.

Nonrecognition was another weapon of intervention advanced by Welles. A poor, imbalanced society, dependent
upon its economic relations with the United States, Cuba
needed recognition. No Cuban government could remain in
power without it, as indicated by President Grau's statement
to Welles in September that everyone in Cuba would support
his new government if the United States recognized it.
Welles ignored Grau's suggestion.[16] He used the fiction of
communist infiltration to convince the State Department
that "it would be highly prejudicial to our interests to intimate in any manner that recognition of the existing regime
was being considered by us."[17] In reality, his concern was for
business interests: "It is also within the bounds of possibility
that the social revolution which is under way cannot be
checked. American properties and interests are being
gravely prejudiced."[18]

The department followed Welles's recommendation not to
recognize the Grau government. The ambassador convinced
Secretary Hull that American relations with Cuba were dic-
tated by economic necessity. He advised Hull, "Our own
commercial interests in Cuba cannot be revived under this

Grau government."[19] And he referred to the connection between Hull's reciprocal trade program and the Cuban market.

At one point, however, Hull feared an adverse Latin American reaction. Just before the Montevideo conference, he wrote to Acting Secretary of State Phillips that a number of South American states were considering joint recognition of the Grau government. Reading between the lines, Phillips surmised that Hull favored extending recognition before the conference convened to protect his good neighbor image.[20] Phillips answered Hull that the Grau regime appeared to be strengthening but pointed out that Welles was arguing that Cuba did not fulfill two necessary prerequisites for recognition: popular support and the ability to maintain law and order. Apparently Phillips was willing to follow Welles's lead despite his own misgivings regarding the ambassador's behavior.[21]

The department was influenced in favor of Welles by Roosevelt support of him. When Roosevelt met with Welles in November 1933 to discuss Cuban-American relations, Welles persuaded the president to make a public statement defending American policy. Some members of the department, sensing that the presidential statement might be interpreted as a direct and obvious attack on Grau, cautioned against the declaration. Nevertheless, the ambassador succeeded in overriding departmental objections, and Roosevelt made the statement supporting Welles's activities in Cuba.[22]

Not satisfied with nonrecognition as a device for removing Grau, the ambassador encouraged the Cuban military leader, Fulgencio Batista, to engineer another coup and bring a "cooperative" government to power. In January 1934, Grau was overthrown and replaced by Carlos Mendieta. Immediately the department reversed its policy. The rapidity with which recognition was urged and extended to Mendieta was a startling contrast to the failure to recognize Grau's government. As early as January 14, 1934, before a new government was actually formed, Jefferson Caffery, the president's personal representative in Cuba, urged recognition.[23] The department agreed, but Roosevelt realized that such immediate action was in bad taste. He suggested that the United States wait until the new government formed a cabinet before extending recognition. The department waited nine days. On January 23, 1934, instructions were sent to recognize the Mendieta government, and American warships were withdrawn from Cuban waters.

The final phase of American relations with Cuba during the first New Deal involved reestablishing profitable commercial relations. In keeping with Hull's philosophy of reciprocity, the State Department advocated abrogation of the Platt Amendment in exchange for a reciprocal trade agreement with Cuba. Both policies crystallized in the spring and summer of 1934. In May the Platt Amendment was abrogated, and in August the United States signed with Cuba the first agreement under the new Trade Agreements Act. Symbolically, Welles and Caffery, two outspoken interventionists, attended the formal signing of the trade agreement.[24]

Relations with Cuba represented the first critical test of the application of the Good Neighbor policy, but Roosevelt, with considerable support from the State Department, was willing to continue the interventionist policies of the past.[25]

As with Cuba, American relations with Liberia during the first Roosevelt administration were interventionist in nature. Here, too, after casting about for ways to influence developments, the administration used a nonrecognition tactic at a critical point, and again economic interests took precedence over all other concerns.

American interest in Liberia dated back to 1819, when Liberia was established as a haven for freed slaves. Hostility to the institution of slavery and pressure from such groups as the American Colonization Society led Congress to pass the African Slave Trade Act of March 3, 1819. The act encouraged the settlement of an area of West Africa by former slaves and provided for an American agent there to receive the emigrants. A few years after the act was passed, increased cotton production made slavery profitable enough to discourage further emigration efforts.[26]

During the latter nineteenth and early twentieth centuries, the United States developed stronger ties with Liberia as a result of threatening encroachments there by France and Great Britain. These European imperial states controlled territory adjacent to Liberia and continually applied pressure for special territorial and economic concessions. The greatest threats to the sovereignty and independence of Liberia after 1870 arose from foreign loans and resulting financial controls. In 1871 and again in 1906, the British government loaned Liberia $500,000 guaranteed by a lien upon the customs revenues of the country. The second loan brought with it a British inspector general of the customs with the power to veto any Liberian expenditures. Consequently, the Liberian government, fearing its sovereignty to be in jeopardy, turned to the United States for help. Ultimately, the American government, under the influence of President William Howard Taft's dollar diplomacy, agreed to help the Liberians. The solution offered was a plan for an international loan in which bankers from the United States, Great Britain, France, and Germany would participate and a customs receivership would be established under American direction.[27] Liberia thus became a financial protectorate of the United States.

After World War I, economic developments in the United States led to a more intense concern with Liberia. During the 1920s, growth of the American automobile industry made rubber one of the most important commodities entering international trade. The sharp increase in the demand for rubber and the relatively limited supply led to the skyrocketing of prices. Great Britain and the Netherlands controlled the rubber market, and opposition to their monopolies arose in the United States, the greatest single market for rubber. American rubber interests, especially the Firestone Tire and Rubber Company, sought to cultivate new producing areas. The search for new sources led Firestone to Liberia, a country ideally suited for growing rubber. In 1924, the company commenced negotiations with the Liberian government.

Difficulties in Liberian-American relations started in 1926, when the Liberians, confronted with a severe economic crisis, leased the Firestone Company a million-acre tract of land for the production of raw rubber, without adequate safeguards for native land and labor. For the lease, Liberia received a $2.5 million loan on the conditions that the Liberians would accept five American financial advisers and that the Firestone Company would have veto power over any new loans for twenty years. In short, the Firestone interests capitalized on Liberian economic distress to gain control over their economy.

Liberia was in economic distress by 1931 in large part as a result of exorbitant financial charges imposed by the Firestone loan contract. As much as 55 percent of the entire government budget went toward the payment of the obligation. The Liberians appealed to the League of Nations for help. That international body proceeded to draw up a plan of assistance which, in effect, aided American business interests, not Liberia. The League Plan of Assistance protected America in many ways. It stipulated that the president of the United States appoint the financial adviser to Liberia and gave him broad powers to ensure the efficient organization and functions of Liberian fiscal services and prompt payments on loans which the state contracted as well as authority to appoint several assistants subject to the approval of the American secretary of state. In short, the financial adviser controlled the Liberian economy. If the Liberians objected to his decisions, they could appeal to the chief adviser, an overall supervisory official appointed by and responsible to the League.[28] Given the enormous power granted to the advisory officials, it is not surprising that the State Department made the League plan the basis of its Liberian policy.[29]

Liberia accepted the League Plan of Assistance in September 1932, but in January 1933, the government, unable to meet its obligations, declared a moratorium on payments and dismissed several American officials. The department immediately expressed dissatisfaction to the League of Nations and received, as might have been predicted, complete support for the American point of view.

The department's response to developments in Liberia was restrained compared with the attitude of President Hoover. When he learned that Liberia had suspended loan payments, Hoover wanted to exert strong pressure, sending a naval force if necessary. Secretary Stimson wanted to avoid strong tactics because of possible adverse foreign opinion and Negro disapproval at home. He convinced the president to continue with the State Department's policy of cooperating with the League.[30] In addition, Stimson recommended sending a special mission to Liberia with instructions to seek a solution that would both maintain U.S. cooperation with League efforts to promote reorganization of the country and protect American business interests. The secretary of state also secured the approval of President-elect Roosevelt for his policy.[31] Thus, with the blessings of both Hoover and Roosevelt, Stimson appointed Major General Blanton Winship and Ellis O. Briggs, a State Department officer, to act as the department's representatives to Liberia.

General Winship, head of the mission, favored a tougher line than the department had pursued. Indicative of his attitude was his handling of negotiations with Liberia's president, Edwin James Barclay, in the early spring of 1933. The Liberian president argued that necessity had prompted his suspension of loan payments. He promised to rectify the situation as soon as possible, but as a precondition for resumption of payments, Barclay wanted financial relief. Winship refused. He maintained that Liberian financial difficulties had resulted from corruption in government and refusal to heed the advice of American fiscal agents. Winship reported the substance of his conversation to the department and made recommendations for action which would amount to United States coercion of the Liberian government. The general suggested that the Firestone interests modify their demands, yet he also suggested that before making any accommodations to Liberia, the department insist that Liberia withdraw the moratorium preliminary to any further discussions. In the event that Barclay refused, Winship requested instructions to tell Barclay that the United States would discontinue its support of the Liberian government. Winship also advised that the Finance Corporation of America, one of Liberia's major creditors, maintain its position with respect to repayment. Should President Barclay remain stubborn and refuse repayment or acceptance of the League plan, the general advised that the department ask American philanthropic organizations to leave Liberia, that force be used to protect American property, and that a public statement be issued, with a view toward compromising the Barclay regime, publicizing Liberia's refusal to cooperate. Winship realized that his recommendation might bring about the collapse of the Barclay government, but he argued that a new administration there would probably be willing to accede to American demands.[32] The State Department favored a more subtle interventionist approach than Winship suggested. Since the League plan supported American demands and amounted to intervention with international sanction, the policy makers in the department preferred to work with the international organization.

Departmental policy became complicated in the spring and summer months of 1933. First, the Firestone Company plagued the department with requests for a modification in American policy, urging more direct intervention in Liberia, even the taking over of that state as the special ward of the United States. Although Firestone appeared to accept the department's "international" solution, policy makers expected the company to resume pressure for direct intervention at some later date.[33] A second complication was the outburst of opinion in the United States against the State Department's handling of Liberia. Negro intellectuals asked the department to abandon the League plan, charging, with justification, that it violated Liberian sovereignty. At the same time, liberal magazines exposed the activities of Firestone and the department.[34] These attacks unnerved department officials.[35] The attacks came very close to the truth—the U.S. government had an informal partnership with Firestone that sacrificed Liberian independence for commercial advantage.

The Liberian situation became more involved in the fall and winter of 1933. President Barclay refused to accept the League plan as long as the question of the chief adviser's nationality remained unsettled. He demanded that no American occupy the post because an American financial adviser and an American chief adviser would give the United States complete control over Liberia. The State Department, frustrated by the total bankruptcy of its diplomacy, struggled to reformulate policy.[36] Finally, department officials realized concessions were necessary and agreed to a chief adviser who was not American if that official's powers were not decreased in any way.[37] Yet, as one official in the department observed, timing was all-important: "If this concession were announced too soon, the Liberians would promptly raise up a new series of objections; if on the other hand, it were delayed too long, there was the twin danger of (a) having the Firestones appear to yield to dictation; or else (b) seeing the League get tired of the problem and give it up in a spirit of defeatism." As a precaution against additional demands, the department instructed the American representative in Geneva to secure international support for closing negotiations with Liberia once the concession on the nationality issue was announced.[38]

In Geneva, the American representative obeyed the letter but not the spirit of the department's command. At the meeting of the League Committee on Liberia, he stated both his own sympathies and the official position of the United States. His personal view, he said, had been that the presence of an American chief adviser "might promote an increase in contributions by various interested organizations in the United States for educational, religious and medical purposes." But, he continued, "the American Government does not maintain that the Chief Adviser should be of American nationality."[39] By making the concession so begrudgingly, the representative succeeded only in antagonizing Liberia.

The Liberian government realized that the concession conceded nothing. According to the League plan, the United States retained control over Liberia's economy regardless of the chief adviser's nationality. Consequently, the Liberians determined to reject the League plan. Given the new turn of events, the department reevaluated its tactics, debating whether it should threaten Liberia into accepting the League plan. Opinion divided on the matter. Some believed that a threat to disassociate the United States from Liberia might invite British and French intervention. Others favored threatening Liberia regardless of the risks. Ultimately, the department decided to embarrass Liberia, if it rejected the League plan, as a more effective and less risky approach.[40]

In 1934 and 1935, the Liberian situation assumed greater importance. Great Britain negotiated a rubber restriction agreement with other nations controlling Far Eastern sources, which caused deep concern to the United States, as the foremost consumer of that vital resource.[41] Liberia was a major source of American rubber, and, most significantly, unlike the practice in the Far East, an American firm extracted the Liberian rubber.

Meanwhile, the League of Nations abandoned Liberia to its fate, which meant, in effect, surrendering that country to the mercy of the United States. Early in 1934, the Liberian government had notified the League that it would accept its assistance plan with certain reservations that would have curtailed the powers of the foreign advisers and protected Liberian sovereignty.[42] The League interpreted acceptance with reservations as de facto rejection.

Events in 1934 generated confusion in the department. Uncertain as to what new tactics to use in view of Liberia's reaction to the League plan, the department stumbled from one technique to another. Policy makers ruled out force, but they felt that something had to be done to prevent British or French intervention. At first the department merely registered its concern and anxiety with the Liberian government. Then it tried bluff, threatening to withdraw financial support if Liberia did not accept the plan without reservations.[43] Liberia remained unmoved. Therefore, as a last-ditch effort to salvage American interests, the department sent Harry McBride, special assistant to the secretary of state, on a mission to negotiate directly with President Barclay.[44]

McBride succeeded in convincing Barclay that Liberia had no alternative. The two worked out a Liberian plan of assistance, which actually incorporated most of the major points the United States had argued for in Geneva.[45] The new plan provided Liberia with a face-saving substitute for the League plan. Yet the department insisted that some objectionable parts of the Liberian plan must be removed before the plan would be accepted.[46] Therefore, on McBride's suggestion, the department decided to withhold formal recognition of the Barclay regime until certain clauses were removed.[47] Liberia capitulated. The Liberian-McBride assistance plan gave the United States complete control over Liberia's economy and much of its governing machinery.[48]

Relations with Cuba and Liberia in the 1930s were a precursor of later United States policy toward the aspirations of underdeveloped countries in Africa, Asia, and Latin America. Robert F. Smith suggests that the reactions of Roosevelt and the State Department to the nationalist strivings in what is now known as the Third World displayed ambivalence toward changes there: "While professing commitment to the ideal of national self-determination the United States has often tended to support the status quo in these areas. . . . One of the major factors behind this status quo policy in regard to underdeveloped areas is the worldwide business interests of the United States."[49]

Clearly, there were alternatives. Ambassador Josephus Daniels recommended announcing the Pan-Americanization of the Monroe Doctrine at the Montevideo conference. The Cuban situation presented another opportunity for the United States to implement his advice to accept the same limitation imposed on Europe to maintain a hands-off policy toward domestic affairs in Latin America. A similar course of action might have been followed in Liberia.[50]

4. Open and Closed Doors: The Far East

Cordell Hull continued without substantial modification the Far Eastern policy of his predecessor, Henry L. Stimson. Hull's inability to pursue a different course of action demonstrates the adverse effects of tradition and bureaucratic control on diplomacy. These influential forces went unnoticed at the time, and speculation about Hull's range of authority was confined to his relationship with the new president. Hull maintained that before 1936 he enjoyed almost total control over foreign policy.[1] If Roosevelt's "bombshell message" to the London economic conference and Raymond Moley's insubordination are regarded as indicative only of a period of adjustment in Hull's association with Roosevelt, then the secretary's self-assessment may be accepted as basically valid. Certainly Hull influenced foreign policy on the issue of central interest to him, the lowering of trade barriers. Aside from commercial matters, however, it is difficult to accept Hull's claim that he directed American diplomacy. On many occasions he surrendered his authority to subordinates, habitually allowing the undersecretary or assistant secretaries to report directly to the president, supposedly to free himself for more urgent matters while enhancing their experience and prestige. As a general rule, Hull's decision making was the product of extensive consultation with his "associates," especially the respective division heads.[2] Thus the paradox of Hull's position in the early New Deal was that he gained freedom from above only to become subservient to judgments from below.

One of the subordinates who influenced Hull was Stanley K. Hornbeck, chief of the Far Eastern Division. Hornbeck remembered that "many people in the State Department 'educated' Mr. Hull on various matters in the field of foreign relations. Therefore you might say that my relationship with Mr. Hull in many contexts was that of an expounder and adviser."[3] Apparently Hornbeck's pedagogy was effective; his recommendations and Hull's decisions often were identical. The advice he offered in response to Japanese military action in Manchuria was to carry on the policy adopted during the Hoover period. Although Hornbeck vacillated when he served under Stimson, alternately suggesting condemnation, acquiescence, and finally nonrecognition, he later consistently urged Hull to resist Japanese ambitions.[4]

An early example of the education Hornbeck provided is found in a long memorandum he submitted in March 1933. He began with the dramatic statement, "A war between Japan and the United States within the next four years is a possibility of such reality that the ... ways and means by which its development into actuality may be combatted need to be given serious and constant consideration." Because he was skeptical about the ability of the United States to do more than hasten or retard the impending clash, Hornbeck recommended following and strengthening the current policy and advised that as long as Japan continued to augment her military power, "we should keep ahead of Japan in that line of endeavor." If Japan persisted with her imperialistic design, Hornbeck suggested cooperation with other nations, particularly League of Nations members, providing the United States was not left out on a limb. He concluded with the observation, "The problem of each Administration in this country is not so much that of deciding what shall be our Far Eastern *policy* as that of developing features of strategy and moving advisedly in the realm of *tactics.*"[5] Throughout the early New Deal Hornbeck submitted variations on this theme, urging preservation of continuity in American Far Eastern policy.

Hornbeck and other senior advisers based their tutorials with Hull upon the teachings of Stimson, the revered master under whom most had served. Stimson's initial reaction to the Manchurian crisis reflected a thorough knowledge of the restrictions upon American action. Stimson was aware of the nation's military weakness, its isolationist sentiment, and the intricacies of developments in Manchuria. Caution and restraint, therefore, characterized his guidance. Gradually his position hardened and solidified when the Japanese army subdued Chinchow, the final step in dominating Manchuria. At that point, after considering various responses, he embraced the nonrecognition approach to Manchuria, a strategy that gained some currency both within and outside the State Department. With the approval of President Hoover, notes were cabled to the American embassies in Tokyo and Nanking for delivery to the respective foreign offices. These messages stated that the United States "cannot admit the legality of any situation *de facto* nor does it intend to recognize any treaty or agreement entered into between those Governments (China and Japan), or agents thereof, which may impair the treaty rights of the United States or its citizens in China . . . and that . . . [the United States] does not intend to recognize any situation, treaty or agreement which may be brought about by means contrary to the . . . Pact of Paris."[6] An expression of blind international legalism, Stimson's nonrecognition pronouncement represented a distorted perception in the State Department of Asian realities in both the Hoover and Roosevelt administrations. Stubborn adherence to nonrecognition in the Manchurian situation, without the military capabilities that might be needed to enforce the policy and without popular support for the policy in the United States, was a singular error.[7]

Shortly after the announcement of the nonrecognition doctrine, Stimson elaborated upon it somewhat obliquely. He wrote to Senator William E. Borah, chairman of the Senate Foreign Relations Committee, on February 23, 1932, with several objectives in mind. He wanted to rouse Britain from her diplomatic slumbers, influence the League of Nations, encourage China, and warn Japan. He expressed the last of these intentions emphatically. The letter threatened a naval build-up beyond treaty limitations and fortification of Pacific islands, also a treaty violation, if other nations failed to abide by the agreements made at the Washington Conference in 1922, which, he asserted, guaranteed to all countries equality of commercial opportunity in China and the sovereignty of that nation. In essence, Stimson reminded Borah, the nation, and foreign powers that the Washington treaties formed "the legal basis upon which now rests the 'open door' policy toward China."[8] Regardless of the merit of Stimson's abstract reasoning, his ideas expressed the Open Door tradition.

After the 1932 presidential election Stimson sought a new constituency for his policy. An invitation by the president-elect on January 9, 1932, provided him with an opportunity to review the Far Eastern situation and persuade Roosevelt to retain the nonrecognition formula. Roosevelt was amenable, and on January 17 he publicly endorsed Stimson's policy. Roosevelt's action surprised some of his closest advisers. Rexford G. Tugwell alerted him to the possibility of war. Roosevelt countered with the remark that such a war might better come sooner than later. Moley also disagreed with the policy but was cut short by Roosevelt's recollection that the president's ancestors had traded with China and the sentiment: "I have always had the deepest sympathy with the Chinese. How could you expect me not to go along with Stimson on Japan?"[9]

Stimson was equally successful in his first encounters with Hull. He recalled that during extended talks with the incoming secretary in the interregnum they agreed on Far Eastern policy. Hull also promised to support the career officers in every way.[10] Similarly, Hull recorded that "Secretary Stimson, in my long conferences with him, had emphasized the policy he was pursuing, of opposing Japan's advance into China by all the diplomatic means at his command, including a refusal to recognize Japan's acquisition of Manchuria. . . . Since Japan's undeclared war in China was in flagrant violation of the Nine-Power treaty signed at Washington in 1922, Mr. Roosevelt and I wanted our statements to reflect our intention to continue unchanged the opposition of this Government to Japan's expanding ambitions."[11] With Roosevelt's and Hull's concurrence assured, Stimson left office in the physical sense only; in spirit he remained.

A concrete expression of Hull's intention to continue Stimson's policy occurred in February 1933. Stimson had worked assiduously to encourage other nations, especially Great Britain, to support the condemnation of Japan. His efforts were rewarded on February 23, 1933, when the League of Nations chastised the Japanese. Two days later Stimson sent a statement to the League joining the United States in the combined censure. As for Hull, he "had no hesitation in agreeing with Stimson on the wording of the message he sent to the League on February 25, 1933, joining in the League's condemnation of Japan's actions."[12] That same month the United States received an invitation from the League to participate in the deliberations of its Advisory Committee, a body responsible for observing Far Eastern developments. In March the invitation was accepted and the United States sent a nonvoting member.

Meanwhile, the British were considering another demonstration of their displeasure with Japan. Prompted by the League's acceptance of the Lytton report and evidence of renewed Japanese military action, political groups in Britain criticized the government for not taking additional steps to curtail the Japanese. They agitated for an arms embargo but disagreed over using the measure as a sanction against Japan or applying it impartially to both belligerents. Responding to the pressure, Sir John Simon notified Parliament on February 27, 1933, that the government would temporarily prohibit munitions shipments to China and Japan pending consultation with other nations interested in an international agreement. Convinced that a multilateral embargo was meaningless without American participation, the British approached Stimson with their scheme. Noting the lack of presidential authority and the absence of department enthusiasm for an impartial embargo, which would only invite retaliation, Stimson discouraged them.[13]

In March 1933, the British introduced a modification of the arms embargo idea at the Geneva Disarmament Conference. The conference was on the verge of collapse, paralyzed by French anxiety that disarmament alone would not protect them against another German invasion. To assuage French fears, the British delegate, Sir Arthur Henderson, proposed a collective security arrangement which included the United States. He envisioned American cooperation with European powers in identifying and punishing the aggressor nation when war occurred. The punishment would take the form of an arms embargo imposed upon the villain. Later the British submitted a more comprehensive security proposal to the conference, the MacDonald Plan, encompassing the arms embargo scheme.

The American representative to the conference, Norman H. Davis, duly reported the British invitation to the State Department and endorsed American acceptance.[14] Hull responded enthusiastically—a bit too enthusiastically to suit many of his subordinates. He wanted to apply the proposal in the Far East, Latin America, and Europe. As he later wrote, "We wanted to leave no doubt that we had Japan in mind as well."[15] Hull was dissuaded, however, by members of the department and by the obvious lack of sympathy on the part of Congress.[16] Hornbeck cautioned the secretary that "an embargo on export of arms to China and/or Japan . . . is a form of sanction, that it may lead to the necessity for employing other forms of sanctions or may bring on acts of retaliation which may lead to war."[17] Ultimately, by passing an impartial embargo bill, Congress made it impossible to use the embargo as a punitive device, and Hull and his colleagues had to resort to less forceful means of discouraging the Japanese.

Undaunted by the attitude of other nations, Japan withdrew from the League and flouted world opinion in other ways. She embarked upon a policy of economic coercion designed to force recognition of her New Order in East Asia. In May 1933, for example, the Japanese government considered either purchasing all foreign petroleum property in Manchuria or implementing a restrictive licensing system on oil importation and refining. Alarmed by the imminent danger to American oil interests, Ambassador Joseph C. Grew reported, "Under either of these plans the foreign oil companies could expect eventually to be driven from the field except for the sale of crude oil. Their distributing plants and organizations in Japan would have to be abandoned."[18] An equally disturbing report reached the State Department in July: the Japanese puppet regime in Manchuria revealed its intention to establish a state-controlled petroleum monopoly, which would endanger British and American oil companies there.[19]

These Japanese assaults upon American oil interests elicited a mixed response from the State Department. Ambassador Grew was conciliatory and merely asked the Japanese Foreign Office to apprise American oil concerns of their business prospects under the anticipated petroleum law in Japan, a modest reaction to a potentially devastating maneuver.[20] Equally solicitous was the recommendation of Stuart J. Fuller, assistant chief of the Far Eastern Division, who advised making representations to the Manchurian government rather than implicating Japan, in effect a surrender to Japanese pressure. Raymond C. McKay, also of the Far Eastern Division, however, argued that protests made to Manchuria only postponed the inevitable; eventually such action would have to be directed at Japan.[21] When Manchuria implemented an oil monopoly in 1934, Hull merely chastised Japan verbally by reasserting the nonrecognition policy, which had no impact on the Japanese.[22]

The Japanese persisted with their abrasive actions in 1934. They waged economic warfare, boldly asserted special rights in East Asia, and disavowed the naval limitation treaties. It was a critical year in relations between Japan and the United States. The year began with a clash between two principal Far Eastern specialists in the State Department,

Hornbeck and Grew, on American policy. The dialogue was generated by Hornbeck's address on January 18 to the Ninth Conference on the Cause and Cure of War. Grew learned from Japanese sources that Hornbeck had said, "I need only call attention to the fact that the formula, or non-recognition, has been employed by the American Government on several occasions. . . . This formula gained worldwide attention when it was invoked by the identic notes addressed by the American Government to the Chinese and Japanese Governments in connection with the developments in Manchuria."[23] Although Grew never disputed the efficacy of the nonrecognition policy, he objected that public declaration of it was unnecessarily provocative.[24] Grew communicated his annoyance to the State Department. The department, in turn, informed him that Hornbeck had not made the statement in question and instructed Grew to clarify the matter with the Japanese. Hornbeck commented: "The simple facts are: the American Government announced in 1932 that it 'did not intend to recognize': maintenance by it of that position calls for no action and no new affirmation."[25] Seemingly a minor confrontation, the argument illuminated a basic disagreement. Hornbeck later remembered that Grew was a "diplomat's diplomat" but that others did not share Grew's faith in diplomacy.[26] Unlike Grew, Hornbeck believed that in view of Japan's intentions, negotiation was useless. Eventually Grew came to share Hornbeck's cynicism.

Diplomatic skepticism in the State Department was undoubtedly the result of frustrating encounters with the Japanese. Japan's discriminatory practices in Manchuria and galling inattention to American remonstrances provoked a search for more persuasive measures. The most intriguing alternative the department found involved action with other similarly disaffected powers. In the summer of 1934, for example, Britain was urged to assume leadership in an Anglo-American rebuke of Japan's actions.[27] Unfortunately, Britain proved to be an elusive ally. She accepted but later declined the invitation. Then Grew developed a more ambitious scheme. Usually cautious, he was emboldened by an awareness that "a very serious issue is at stake, involving in large degree the future of our commercial interests and our traditional policy in the Far East."[28] Therefore, he suggested that the department consider, in consultation with Britain, placing a partial or total embargo on crude oil shipments to Japan. The department concurred but modified Grew's recommendation in two ways: the Netherlands would be asked to participate, and precautions would be taken to prevent the United States from being stranded by its allies.[29] Acting Secretary of State Phillips instructed Grew to encourage representatives from those nations to initiate the action and to express American willingness to collaborate in the venture. Neither power responded, and the plan was abandoned.[30]

One of the more startling events of 1934 occurred on April 17. A spokesman for the Japanese Foreign Office, Eliji Amau, stated: "Owing to the special position of Japan in her relations with China, her views and attitude respecting matters that concern China, may not agree in every point with those of foreign nations; but it must be realized that Japan is called upon to exert the utmost effort in carrying out her mission and in fulfilling her special responsibilities in East Asia."[31] Although there was some confusion at first as to exactly what Amau had said, and why he had said it, the State Department concluded that Japan was alerting foreign powers that they must maintain a hands-off policy in China.[32] Some officials believed the statement might have been prompted by Japanese resentment over recent American assistance to China, which included a wheat and cotton loan and the presence of American aviators there.[33]

The text of the reply to the Amau pronouncement stimulated some controversy in the State Department. Hornbeck instructed his assistants in the Far Eastern Division to draft a note "which was effectively declarative and at no point vulnerable to a cavilling rejoinder by the Japanese Government nor from any quarter."[34] Other department members, including Hornbeck's colleagues in the division, disagreed and suggested a less harsh reply.[35] Hornbeck ignored them.

On April 28, 1934, Grew was told to present an aide memoire
to the Japanese Foreign Office which affirmed that "no nation can, without the assent of other nations concerned,
rightfully endeavor to make conclusive its will in situations
where there are involved the rights, the obligations and the
legitimate interests of other sovereign states."[36] Most senior
department members, including Grew and Hull, were
pleased with the document, an indication that American
policy, in not recognizing Manchukuo, would remain unchanged.[37]

Shortly after the Amau declaration, Japan underlined
her hegemonic aspirations in China. On May 16, 1934, Ambassador Hirosi Saito met Hull privately to discuss ways of
ameliorating the tension between his country and the
United States. He presented Hull with an eight-point memorandum. The seventh point revealed Japan's intention. It
proposed a joint declaration in which Japan and the United
States pledged to cooperate on the promotion of commercial
equality, respect each other's territorial possessions, and
recognize Japan's special responsibilities in the western Pacific and the United States' responsibilities in the eastern
Pacific. Hull rejected Saito's offer because it violated the
Open Door principle.[38]

In retrospect, Hull commented that Saito's proposal "was
a start along the line of later Japanese propaganda that
what she wanted was a 'Monroe Doctrine' in the Far East
pretendedly such as our Monroe Doctrine for the Western
Hemisphere." He regarded the claim as a fraudulent misrep-
resentation which ignored the defensive nature of the
American doctrine and merely disguised Japan's imperialistic ambitions.[39] His judgment was shared by his colleagues.
Grew made an identical observation in his memoirs, and
Hornbeck had formed the same view long before either Hull
or Grew did.[40] These architects of Far Eastern policy may
have misread history. The corollaries to the Monroe Doctrine in the nineteenth and early twentieth centuries suggest that there was some historical merit to Japanese
pretensions.

Japan's aggressive rhetoric in 1934, amplified by an announcement that Japan would terminate its adherence to the naval limitation treaties of 1922 and 1930, drove the State Department to the crossroads of decision. The alternatives to nonrecognition had to be explored. The signs pointed to either recommending withdrawal from the Far East or insisting upon the maintenance of American rights and interests in that area. Grew identified the options in precisely that way in December, and, because the administration was already on the road to resisting Japan, he urged an acceleration in naval preparedness. Invoking past diplomacy, Grew averred: "Theodore Roosevelt enunciated the policy of 'Speak softly but carry a big stick.' If our diplomacy in the Far East is to achieve favorable results, and if we are to reduce the risk of an eventual war with Japan to a minimum, that is the only way to proceed."[41]

Hull's recollection of the available alternatives to nonrecognition was identical to Grew's. The secretary remembered:

> We were now at the Oriental crossroads of decision. There were two courses open to us. One was to withdraw gradually, perhaps with dignity, from the Far East. . . . The other was to continue to insist on the maintenance of law, on our legitimate rights and interests in the Far East, and on observance of the treaties and declarations that guaranteed an independent China and pledged equality to all nations, nonintervention, nonaggression, and peaceful settlement of disputes in the Orient.[42]

Hull and Roosevelt chose the second course, to reaffirm U.S. "rights," but that course necessitated military preparedness, which they did not implement until much later. So, in effect, the administration continued to adhere to nonrecognition as its policy for the Far East.

Hornbeck once again preceded both Hull and Grew on policy judgments. He wrote in May 1934: "The most effective step that can be taken by the present Administration in this

country toward making our position in relation to Far Eastern questions what it should be lies in the direction of bend-
ing this country's energy toward the building up of a
definitely 'superior' U.S. Navy."[43] Several dissident officials
in the department argued that the nation was heading in the
wrong direction. Edwin L. Neville, counselor of the American Embassy in Japan, and Eugene H. Dooman, an officer in
the Far Eastern Division, favored withdrawal.[44] They were
virtually ignored.

At various points in 1935 and 1936, Grew privately admitted his agreement with the department dissidents. He
recorded in his diary in January 1935 that Japan's popula-
tion growth and legitimate aspiration for a higher standard
of living necessitated foreign trade. Given the high tariff
walls built by Western nations, if these powers also blocked
Japanese commercial dominance in the Far East, Japan
would fight rather than starve. "Unless Japan is given sympathetic cooperation in her economic difficulties—which of
course are at the root of all the political trouble—there is
bound to be an explosion or a series of explosions (of which
the Manchurian affair was one) in due course." In February
1936, he recorded his dissatisfaction with the obsolete Nine
Power Treaty and belief that a bilateral agreement of limited duration with Japan would afford better protection of
American interests and possibly avoid a naval race. But
Japan must be made aware of American intentions—accom-
modation did not mean withdrawal.[45]

Hornbeck and other highly placed officials had no second
thoughts about American policy.[46] Hornbeck repeatedly defended the U.S. diplomatic reaction to Far Eastern developments as the expression of two general principles of
American foreign policy: commercial equality and the right
of sovereign states to remain free. Contemporary Asian solutions to their economic problems, he believed, challenged
those basic premises. "Thus in connection with China," he
argued, "there had developed a particular application of the
principle of equality of opportunity and there has come
about the use of the expression 'open door policy.' As a mat-

ter of fact the expression 'open door' might more accurately be coupled with the designation 'doctrine.' "[47]

Grew's brief departure from orthodox policy ended in 1936 when Japan instituted a domestic petroleum control law. In August he recommended "adequate naval preparedness on the part of our country to meet at any moment, now and in the future, unforeseen developments in the Far East which might lead us, contrary to all calculations and policies, into war with Japan."[48] By the end of the early New Deal, every major figure in the State Department who was involved in Far Eastern policy had reached agreement on the proper course to follow.

Early New Deal domestic experimentation was not matched by similar eclecticism in Far Eastern policy. Hull and his colleagues never paused at the "Oriental crossroads of decision" in 1934. They chose the same route Stimson had chosen and went no further. Like Stimson, Hull advocated the maintenance of commercial equality and Chinese sovereignty, both integral parts of the Nine Power Treaty and the Open Door tradition. Unable to use any coercive measures, Hull upheld the nonrecognition doctrine in Manchukuo, ignoring Japanese pressures. The State Department, to its credit, came to realize that the nonrecognition policy was ineffective. But arguments for building up U.S. naval power in 1934 and later represented a curious inversion of diplomatic logic. The cardinal principle of diplomacy—resist when strong—became resist, then strengthen. That acrobatic thinking might have been plausible if Congress had been equally nimble. It was not; isolationism prevailed. Thus the State Department tied itself in a political knot by adopting a view that presupposed the exercise of military power for which there was no popular support. Unaware of the extent of their failure, Hull and most of his subordinates had few misgivings. Withdrawal, accommodations, and bilateral negotiation with Japan were never given serious consideration except for the momentary private conjectures of Grew and the public complaints of several lesser lights in the department.

Hull's failure to pursue alternatives to a demonstrably bankrupt policy cannot be explained simply. His inexperience in foreign affairs and awe of professional diplomats, his sensitivity to domestic pressures, his occasional difficulties with the president and presidential advisers, and his preoccupation with commercial matters detracted from Hull's ability to change Asian policy. Occasionally on other issues, notably the battle for lower tariffs, he exhibited the determination necessary to redirect the course of foreign policy. Unfortunately, his monistic view of international relations, in which he reduced all problems to the deleterious effects of worldwide economic competition, and his single-minded determination to excoriate that assumed evil, distracted Hull. He delegated far too much authority to his associates in Asian matters, and his deference to them was surpassed only by their slavish devotion to Stimson's views and the Open Door tradition.

Hull and his colleagues recognized that the country was at the crossroads of a major decision. They knew one choice involved acting more forcefully toward Japan and preparing militarily to curtail Japanese expansion. They also knew that an alternative choice meant acquiescing to Japanese expansion. Either of these decisions would have been better than the policy they recommended. They simply proclaimed the liberal principles that underlay American foreign policy.[49] As a result, American policy reached a dead end.

5. Collective Security

The degree to which members of the State Department accepted the principle of collective security is open to question. Historian Robert A. Divine called attention to the issue in an investigation of the arms embargo debate of 1933. He noted that aside from their analyses of major events, historians have neglected Franklin D. Roosevelt's foreign policy before 1937. Divine sought to fill the void by concentrating on Roosevelt's attitude toward collective security as revealed by the president's action during the arms embargo controversy in 1933. Before offering his own evaluation of Roosevelt's position, Divine commented on two earlier, opposed accounts of the subject: Charles A. Beard's *American Foreign Policy in the Making* and Basil Rauch's *Roosevelt from Munich to Pearl Harbor.* He found that "in both accounts, the villains are easy to identify. For Beard, they are the internationalists who conspired unsuccessfully to lead the President away from an isolationist policy; for Rauch the Senate is to blame for destroying a promising movement toward collective security." Divine set out to prove that the embargo controversy and the president's attitude were not as simple or as clearcut as Beard and Rauch implied. Divine partially agreed with Beard's contention that Roosevelt would not deviate from the isolationist position he adopted in 1932 when he repudiated the League; but he suggested that Roosevelt's concern for domestic reform probably governed his decision to disavow collective security in the early 1930s.[1]

Although Divine denied any intention of singling out martyrs, heroes, and villains, two personalities appear more heroic than others in his study: Secretary of State Hull and his confidant, Ambassador Norman H. Davis. Noting the strong resurgence of internationalism in the State Department, he concluded that "the strength of the Wilsonian tradition, embodied in the sincere efforts of men like Hull and Davis, could not dissolve the grip of isolation on the people, the Congress, and the President."[2] Divine's comments regarding Beard's and Rauch's treatment of Roosevelt's position apply to his own analysis of Hull and Davis. Their position was not as simple or clear-cut as Divine implies. There is evidence that Hull, Davis, and many other members of the State Department were interested neither in the arms embargo per se nor in collective security.

As originally conceived by internationalists in the Hoover period, the arms embargo was designed to involve the United States in collective security efforts.[3] The Sino-Japanese military confrontation in Manchuria in 1931 forced the question of America's reaction to breaches of the peace, and Congress devised arms embargo schemes directed at that conflict. Faced with economic collapse at home, President Hoover sought to avoid involvement in the Far East. Similarly, Hoover's secretary of state, Henry Stimson, initially rejected the arms embargo approach but then recommended greater cooperation with the League of Nations by refusing to interfere with any sanctions which that organization might adopt against the Japanese.[4] In November 1931, despite the president's cool response to his ideas, Stimson informed the American representative attending the League Council meetings that the United States, though unable to participate in an embargo against Japan, would not hinder League activity.

The Manchurian crisis intensified in 1932, and Stimson advised American cooperation in applying economic sanctions against Japan. Hoover refused. The United States confined its policy to moral sanctions, announcing the nonrecognition doctrine. As the Manchurian crisis deepended, American public opinion was aroused. China had a special place in the hearts of Americans. The dream of a potential market for American goods, culture, and political institutions was a striking feature of the attitude toward China in the late nineteenth and early twentieth centuries. The attachment to China, undiminished when Hoover became president, prompted criticism of the weak policy adopted toward Japan. Congress took the lead in translating sentiment into legislative action. In December 1931, Representative Morton Hull introduced a resolution to embargo all trade to any nation violating the Kellogg-Briand Pact. He withdrew the bill after Secretary Stimson informed the House Foreign Affairs Committee that he considered the resolution inadvisable at that moment. Stimson's statement reflected the attitude of President Hoover; Stimson did not oppose the basic intent of Representative Hull's proposal.

The Chaco War broke out between Bolivia and Paraguay in the summer of 1932 and provided Stimson with another opportunity to pursue a stronger policy toward aggressor powers. In December 1932, Stimson recommended that the administration ask for discretionary executive authority to embargo arms to countries where hostilities existed or were threatened. By allowing the president to determine the aggressor, the Stimson proposal added a formidable weapon to the chief executive's diplomatic arsenal. Hoover endorsed Stimson's suggestion with great reluctance, and even the secretary's colleagues in the department raised objections. Undersecretary of State William Castle notified Stimson of his opposition, pointing out that the munitions industry would create a furor. Events proved Castle to be right. News of the arms embargo plan leaked to the press, and Hoover, bombarded with protests from the munitions industry, decided against sending Stimson's request to Congress.

Nevertheless, when Stimson again raised the arms embargo idea in January 1933, some of those who had previously expressed doubts reversed their position. Undersecretary Castle changed his mind and supported the measure, and Hoover endorsed it as a last resort. Hoover preferred requesting the Senate to ratify the 1925 Geneva Convention for the control of the arms trade and presenting the arms embargo only if the Senate refused. On January 10, the administration sent a new version of the Stimson resolution to Congress.

After Congress received the arms embargo resolution, William E. Borah, chairman of the Senate Foreign Relations Committee, invited Undersecretary Castle to attend an executive session of the committee. Castle, Francis White, assistant secretary for Latin American affairs, and Joseph C. Green, the author of Hoover's message embodying the Stimson approach, attended the meeting. The department officers stated that the embargo would apply to the Chaco War, not the Far Eastern war. Relieved that the proposed embargo would not implicate the United States in the Manchurian affair, the Senate committee agreed to report out the administration bill immediately. Senator Borah presented the resolution on January 19 and succeeded in obtaining senatorial consent for adoption without debate. On the following day Hiram Bingham of Connecticut, a senator from a state that had a large munitions industry, blocked final passage by moving for reconsideration of the measure. Under a Senate rule, Bingham's action prevented adoption without full-scale debate. Borah asked Bingham to drop his motion, but Bingham refused and mustered sufficient support to prevent Borah from bringing up the resolution for adoption.

The State Department then shifted its appeal to the House and persuaded Representative Samuel D. McReynolds, chairman of the House Foreign Affairs Committee, to present the bill. Department officials assured McReynolds that the legislation applied only to the Chaco War. Meanwhile, the situation in the Far East had deteriorated further, and the League, as a result of the Lytton Commission findings, had condemned the Japanese for aggression in Manchuria. McReynolds, acutely aware of the implications of the Far Eastern crisis, told the House Foreign Affairs Committee that war would immediately ensue if Congress passed the embargo resolution. By way of compromise, McReynolds agreed to accept the embargo resolution if it contained an amendment limiting its scope to the Western

Hemisphere. Stimson was annoyed and told a fellow department official that such an amendment would destroy the solid front he had built against Japan. Apparently, the secretary had allowed his subordinate to present the embargo as a measure directed at the Chaco War, while he envisioned wider usage. In any case, Congress failed to act, and the bill remained in limbo.

When the arms embargo issue reemerged, it was closely related to other foreign policy issues—European disarmament, the London economic conference, the Far Eastern situation, and Latin American peace—as well as to the domestic crisis. For this reason, the State Department subordinated the arms embargo measure, with its timid promise to aid European security, to what were regarded as more urgent concerns.

At the beginning of the Roosevelt administration, members of the department expressed fears and reservations regarding the implementation of the arms embargo measure. Aware of the possible Japanese reaction to embargo legislation, Hornbeck urged in a memorandum on March 7, 1933, that the resolution should specifically exclude the Far East.[5] The following week, Hornbeck recommended an alternative to the arms embargo approach. He argued that because a war with Japan was possible within four years, the United States should strengthen itself and advise other governments of a mutuality of interests in the Far East:

> Our efforts therefore should be directed toward strengthening ourselves.... [with] military preparations.... At the same time ... we should keep constantly in our minds and in those of other governments the idea of coincidence of interest and ... should cultivate the spirit and practice of cooperation.[6]

Despite Hornbeck's qualification that the United States reserve the right to decide when combined action in the Far East was in the nation's interest, his attitude toward collective security was far in advance of the views expressed by other department officials, who envisioned the arms embargo as a substitute for military force. Moreover, those officials who advocated embargo legislation urged that its scope be confined to the Western Hemisphere and Europe, a device to promote Latin American peace and European disarmament. Jay Pierrepont Moffat, chief of the division of Western European Affairs, summarized the State Department's views: "Norman Davis, the Latin American Division and ourselves are very anxious to see it put through though it should not be used in the present Far Eastern crisis. It can, however, be applied usefully in Latin America and its existence would be of great help to Norman Davis and his disarmament."[7] Even Joseph C. Green, a strong advocate of the embargo bill, regarded it not as a tactic to outflank European critics but as a counter to those who might charge that the United States by its uncooperative action frustrated peace efforts. He wrote a memorandum documenting a conversation with a congressman: "If this resolution were not passed, certain European governments would succeed in making it appear that the League of Nations was prepared to impose embargoes, and that it was prevented from doing so by the failure of this Government to obtain authority from Congress to cooperate with it."[8] No one in the department viewed the arms embargo as the beginning of increased activity in the field of collective security.

Secretary of State Hull's attitude toward the arms embargo and collective security must be examined in the context of his general attitude toward the problem of world peace. As a legislator, he had expressed his belief that the major causes of war were economic.[9] At the end of World War I, for example, he praised the third of Wilson's Fourteen Points, which provided for the removal of trade restrictions and the promotion of commercial equality in the international market: "The subject matter of this proposal is of the broadest and most far-reaching nature, and upon the solution of the extremely vital problems it presents measurably depend the peace and friendship of nations. Instead of vainly striving to prevent wars after the causes have once arisen, this proposal has for its purpose the prevention of many causes of war."[10] Hull's belief in the connection between trade and war was reinforced with the onset of the depression, when he feared that the chaotic economic situation would lead to an eventual military conflict.[11]

On the first day of the Roosevelt administration, Hull told Feis, the department's expert on economic affairs, that throughout his official life he had tried to persuade his fellow legislators that trade barriers between nations not only promoted economic injury but represented one of the prime causes of war.[12] In drafting the Democratic platform, Hull had been reluctant to go beyond the vague security plank and had focused his attention on international trade.[13] His solution to the problems of peace and economic dislocation was commercial equality among nations, a program he fought for at the very same time the arms embargo resolution was being considered. Hull did support the arms embargo, but his support was not prompted by any desire for collective security; rather, he believed European powers would sympathize with his trade program at the forthcoming economic conference if the United States indicated some willingness to cooperate with European security efforts.

While Congress and the State Department considered the arms embargo resolution, European developments heightened the international consequences of American action or inaction. The Geneva Disarmament Conference was about to fail in the spring of 1933. France, with the largest army in Europe, refused to disarm unless she received promises of assistance from Great Britain and the United States if Germany attacked again. Great Britain, although sympathetic to France's security problem, would not make any guarantees without comparable action by the United States. In March, Britain attempted to break the impasse with new proposals. Arthur Henderson, the British delegate, suggested American participation in collective security. He envisioned an arrangement whereby the United States would consult with European states when aggression occurred, and, if agreement were reached as to the identity of the aggressor, the United States would cooperate by not supplying the guilty party with war materiel. Shortly thereafter, the British presented their prime minister's comprehensive MacDonald Plan. The crucial section on security reiterated the essence of Henderson's recommendation.

As the American representative to the Geneva Disarmament Conference and as one who had access to Secretary Hull, Ambassador Davis was extremely important.[14] Davis expressed his views on the MacDonald Plan in three dispatches on April 16, 1933. In the first he wrote, "As a practical matter I see no reason why we should not limit our undertaking to non-interference with collective action resulting from a continental European agreement assuming, of course, that we concur." Davis elaborated in a second dispatch, which expressed the true intent of his initial recommendation: "If, however, we have contractual relationships which clearly point out our duty, and if with the approbation and sanction of the States concerned this duty is restricted and limited to certain passive action, *then it would seem that we stand a better chance of keeping our country from being dragged into the melee.*" This second communication explained how the MacDonald Plan might insulate the United States from European political problems. His advice belied any attachment to the principle of collective action as an end in itself. In the third dispatch, he attempted to convince Hull of the wisdom of acceding to the MacDonald Plan by stressing the relationship between the Geneva Disarmament Conference and the forthcoming London economic conference: "To create a basis for successful work at Geneva and to use every effort toward the ultimate success of the Economic Conference, I am convinced that is essential to bring about a political appeasement between the European powers."[15] Hull's initial response to Davis's argument was positive.[16]

Davis also urged that the United States insist that its cooperation with European security be contingent upon disarmament. In a memorandum he wrote: "We certainly should not allow ourselves to be put in the position where the responsibility would fall upon us for deciding whether or not collective action should be taken against the violator.... I am inclined to believe that the wiser course would be for us to reiterate our position with regard to disarmament."[17] Davis's all-embracing preoccupation with disarmament prompted his sponsorship of very modest cooperation in collective security to achieve what he considered to be the major objective of American foreign policy in Europe.[18]

The Davis dispatches deeply impressed Hull. He transmitted Davis's suggestions to Roosevelt and formulated instructions. When Prime Minister MacDonald visited Roosevelt on April 23, 1933, Roosevelt, without consulting the department, told the prime minister that he approved the MacDonald Plan in its entirety, including the collective security provisions of Part I. Three days later he made a similar commitment to French Premier Edouard Herriot. Consequently, when instructions to Davis were drafted, the assurances to both MacDonald and Herriot were incorporated. In addition, Hull expressed disagreement with Davis's recommendations for a policy of regional treatment, a fundamental aspect of the department's thinking on the matter up to this time, instructing him to press for a universal disarmament treaty.[19]

The reaction to Hull's instructions by subordinate members of the department was immediate and unsympathetic. When they received the secretary's draft of his instruction to Davis, Moffat and Phillips pointed out to Hull that Part I of the MacDonald Plan would involve the United States far deeper in collective security than was desirable.[20] Hull ignored their advice and sent his instructions to Davis. When Davis received Hull's instructions, he telegraphed Hull reaffirming his belief in a regional approach to disarmament and a much more limited commitment to collective security: "I should be disposed to limit the effectiveness only to the case of an aggressor determined among the continental states of Europe with which decision we independently concurred.... Complete independence of action and of judgment would ... seem desirable as regards the American

Continents, the Far East or our relations with England."[21] At that point, Roosevelt and Hull were advocating policies that discounted the reservations expressed by department officials who supported the arms embargo and arms limitation.[22]

On May 22, 1933, Davis formally announced American policy on collective security at the Geneva conference:

> In the event that the states, in conference, determine that a state has been guilty of a breach of the peace in violation of international obligations and take measures against the violator, then, if we concur in the judgment rendered as to the responsible and guilty party, we will refrain from any action tending to defeat such collective effort which these states may thus make to restore peace.[23]

American adherence to collective security depended upon the signing of a genuine disarmament agreement. Moreover, the promise was limited. The United States merely agreed to refrain from interference in collective action against an aggressor if the United States government agreed that the party designated was guilty. After Davis delivered his speech, he clarified America's position before members of the press. A memorandum summarized the press conference as follows: "A correspondent appeared to be concerned lest the United States was committing itself too far in the matter of security. Mr. Davis told him not to worry. The United States was not making a commitment. The unilateral declaration we may make is clearly contingent on general disarmament."[24] Davis's remarks at Geneva did not represent a fundamental change in the American attitude toward collective security.[25] The State Department eschewed political entanglements with Europe and advised a careful definition of the conditions under which the United States might cooperate in security matters.

The department's reaction to British and French pressures for greater American involvement in European security also reflected a desire to avoid political association with Europe. The British government, anxious to deemphasize the possibilities for success without America's help, indicated it would go no further than the United States in creating a European security program. France attempted to bring the United States closer to European security by introducing a plan in May that linked the United States with League machinery in punishing an aggressor. Typical of the department's reaction to these developments was that of Moffat, who noted in his diary: "The Continentals are still trying to tie us more closely than we are willing to be tied to the scheme of security . . . the British are now joining with them saying that either we must go further in specifying on what basis we will define aggression, or else they will back water and edge out of definite European commitments."[26] Collective security remained a strictly secondary consideration in departmental thinking.

The State Department's response to collective action remained the same in the fall of 1933, with the notable exception of Norman Davis. On October 16, 1933, Phillips, Moffat, and Hull met and decided to clarify and publicize the fact that the United States agreed with European powers on disarmament matters and not political commitments. Moffat recorded, "Norman Davis' telegram indicated that he agreed with this point of view but then proceeded to discuss possibilities of various forms of action in such terms as to lead us to feel that he did not have an attitude quite as aloof as ours."[27] That same day Moffat drew up instructions, approved by Phillips, Hull, and Roosevelt, notifying Davis that the United States was in Geneva only for disarmament purposes.[28]

Arms embargo legislation and European disarmament continued to be subjects of departmental concern in 1934. During that year, Congress passed the antiembargo bill with an amendment fundamentally changing the character of the original resolution. The amendment, presented by Hiram Johnson in May 1933, required impartial application to all belligerents. Johnson transformed the resolution from one of limited cooperation with collective security into a device for remaining completely aloof from threats to world peace. The bill with the Johnson amendment conflicted with the government's policy announced by Davis in Geneva.[29] As a result, most members of the department opposed the Johnson amendment. Their objections were not derived from any firm belief in collective security, however, for, as Moffat observed, the arms embargo was "but one phase, and a relatively small one, of a much larger picture. If [the original resolution were] defeated, it would destroy Mr. Davis' offer and with it much of our disarmament policy." Davis shared Moffat's opinion. According to Moffat, "His feelings too were that a decision as to the Resolution [should be made] not on its own merits but on the basis of a broader picture."[30]

Given the favorable attitude of Congress toward the arms embargo bill, Davis suggested an alternative. He advised that the United States could guarantee execution of the disarmament treaty in such a way as not to interfere with the collective security efforts of the European powers. Moffat objected to Davis's idea on the grounds that it appeared to go farther than the original promise made at Geneva in May 1933. Davis also warned that in the near future the British and French would confront the United States on collective security. His warnings and recommendations were ignored. Moffat and Hull, sensing that Davis was exceeding his instructions, decided to recall him for consultation.[31]

State Department officials continued to endorse a regional approach to the arms embargo and related security issues in the spring of 1934. Renewed interest in the Chaco War led the department to consider applying the arms embargo with the Johnson amendment to that dispute. But they believed such a recommendation would compromise Davis's position in Geneva. Ad hoc embargo legislation to deal with the Chaco question was suggested as an alternative. But Hull and Roosevelt had a different solution. Although Hull had originally objected to the bill with the Johnson amendment, he now wanted a general embargo applying to both belligerents in the Chaco War. President

Roosevelt shared the secretary's opinion and issued a proclamation making it illegal to sell arms to either Bolivia or
Paraguay. Moffat recorded in his diary after Roosevelt's announcement, "This marks a large step forward in our foreign
policy."[32] Indeed, even those officials who at first had objected to the embargo with the Johnson amendment now
accepted it. Their endorsement of the amended bill represented a basic change in attitude.

The State Department's attitude toward collective security was again dramatized in the fall of 1934, when Maxim
Litvinoff, the Russian ambassador at Geneva, advocated a
permanent peace conference with American participation.
When Davis heard the proposal, he wrote Hull: "We have
advocated a General Disarmament Agreement and have
worked earnestly to make a success of the Disarmament
Conference. We have, however, refused in connection with
disarmament, to participate in political discussion and con-
troversies in Europe."[33] Davis clearly lacked interest in combined action to promote peace. He supported the arms
embargo and at times other more ambitious policies solely
to encourage European disarmament.

The real significance of the arms embargo issue lies in its
relative insignificance. Never viewed in isolation, the embargo was always considered in the context of other, more
important, problems by department officials. Thus they expressed a variety of opinions, disagreements emerged, and
positions changed. Hull and Davis, regarded by Divine as
Wilsonian internationalism personified, exemplified intradepartmental vacillation and debate over the embargo
question. Although both men supported a very limited commitment to collective security, each continued to admonish
the other toward a more restrained response. In a sense,
Divine's explanation of Roosevelt's ultimate rejection of the
original embargo illuminates the positions of Hull and Davis
as well. Like Roosevelt, they were preoccupied with other
matters. Hull's answer to the problems of world peace and
economic rehabilitation at home was to liberalize international commerce. His battle for lower tariffs in 1933 and

1934 contrasts strikingly with his minor skirmish over the arms embargo. On the other hand, Davis zealously pursued disarmament. He supported collective security and the embargo only to the extent that those policies promoted his cause. If any unanimity existed in the department regarding the arms embargo, it was the conviction that the embargo should not inaugurate greater American participation in collective security.[34]

6. The Response to Neutrality Legislation

The State Department's attitudes on the arms embargo issue and on neutrality legislation were closely related. In both, the department revealed its intention to promote European peace and prevent American involvement in another European war. Although disagreements persisted among department officials concerning the efficacy of neutrality legislation, they supported a discretionary neutrality bill. Their reservations centered on the rigid and automatic character of congressional proposals and not on the neutrality principle. In particular, the State Department wanted to maintain executive discretion in applying the provisions of such legislation. The department endorsed a neutrality bill, but this action did not represent, as one historian argues, either a drift toward isolation or a radical change in department policy.[1] The State Department continued to work primarily for European peace based on disarmament, as it had in the case of the arms embargo question.

Unlike the arms embargo bill, the administration did not initiate neutrality legislation. The impetus for such a law originated with various peace societies and was furthered by journalistic allegations in exposures about America's entrance into World War I. After the Great War, the peace movement in the United States gained momentum, and, while older, more conservative associations, such as the American Peace Society and the World Peace Foundation, still flourished, they were surpassed by new groups originating at the end of World War I.

These newer organizations differed from the older ones, which operated through their highly placed members and favored educational techniques, by advocating that the United States isolate itself from future wars. The newer organizations, such as the National Council for the Prevention of War and the Women's International League for Peace and Freedom, propagandized to arouse public opinion. They lobbied in Congress, organized mass rallies, and circulated petitions. Frederick J. Libby of the National Council for the Prevention of War and Dorothy Detzer of the Women's International League for Peace and Freedom operated on the premise that armaments caused wars and campaigned for peace through disarmament.[2] Detzer began a crusade to secure a congressional investigation of the American munitions industry,[3] which she believed was responsible for the apparent failure of the Geneva Disarmament Conference.

Detzer won the support of several major peace societies and obtained the help of Senator George W. Norris, with whom she approached Senator Gerald P. Nye and found him enthusiastic. On February 8, 1934, Nye introduced a resolution calling for an investigation of the munitions industry; however, his colleagues were unsympathetic and the measure was promptly referred, first to the Senate Foreign Relations Committee, then to the Military Affairs Committee, with the intention of burying it.[4]

The proposed investigation of the arms industry might have died if it had not been for a sudden outpouring of books and articles on the international arms trade, including *Merchants of Death* by Helmuth C. Engelbrecht and F. C. Hanighen and *Iron, Blood, and Profits* by George Seldes. The authors of *Merchants of Death* described the munitions makers as "one of the most dangerous factors in world affairs." Seldes went further: "The first real step toward that end (peace) is the destruction of the world-wide munitions racket."[5] *Fortune* magazine published an anonymous article entitled "Arms and the Men" in March 1934, which proclaimed: "Without a shadow of a doubt there is at the moment in Europe a huge and subversive force that lies behind

the arming and counterarming of nations: there are mines,
smelters, armament works, holding companies, and banks,
entangled in an international embrace yet working inevita-
bly for the destruction of such little internationalism as the
world has achieved so far."[6] All these publications had one
common element—the belief that munitions makers conspired to promote war.

The journalistic exposures helped crystallize public opinion in favor of the Nye resolution.[7] The peace groups, seeing
an opportunity to promote their cause, began an all-out
effort to win Senate approval of the investigation resolution.
They succeeded. Spurred by popular support, Nye introduced his resolution establishing the Senate investigation of
the munitions industry and the Senate endorsed his recommendation.

The Nye investigating committee presented a serious
problem for the Roosevelt administration. The committee
was dominated by isolationists and sought to prove that the
armaments industry would involve the United States in future wars if not checked by legislative action. Roosevelt did
not share the committee's view and favored dealing with the
arms problem through international cooperation, a position
endorsed by the State Department. But public opinion supported the Nye committee, and Roosevelt had to go along
with the people. Therefore, Roosevelt, like Hoover before
him, suggested that the Senate approve the 1925 Geneva
Arms Convention. But he did not voice objections to the
Senate investigation. The government was following two
diametrically opposed programs for the control of the arms
trade, one favored by the Senate committee and the other
favored by the State Department.[8]

Before the Nye committee was organized, the State Department had recommended an international agreement for
the control of the arms trade and a policy of disarmament.
In 1934, partly in reaction to public opinion but mainly out
of disgust with lack of progress at the Geneva Disarmament
Conference, the department began to support neutrality legislation. Although the conversion was not complete, by the

end of 1935 most officials favored such legislation in some form.

In April 1934, Charles Warren, a distinguished international lawyer who served as attorney general before America's entrance into World War I, published an article in *Foreign Affairs,* "Troubles of a Neutral," based upon a paper he had read to the Council on Foreign Relations in January 1934. Warren recommended that the United States adopt a strict neutrality code to prevent commercial and financial contact with foreign wars. He wrote: "In the future, in order to keep out of war, it will be necessary ... for the United States to do far more than merely comply with its legal obligations of neutrality. In order to avoid friction and complications with the belligerents, it must be prepared to impose upon the actions of its citizens greater restrictions than international law requires." Warren suggested that the administration endorse legislation embracing the following twelve points: (1) prohibition against the use of radio instruments by any belligerent ship in American waters; (2) proscription against the supply or sale of arms and ammunition to all belligerents; (3) provision against the use of American ships for carrying arms and munitions to all belligerents and provision preventing American citizens from traveling or serving on such ships, belligerent or domestic, which carry arms and munitions; (4) preventing the entrance into American ports or waters of any commercial ship of an armed belligerent and forbidding Americans from traveling or serving on such ships; (5) empowering the president to forbid the entrance of belligerent ships flying American colors; (6) preventing the entrance of prizes into American ports; (7) provision barring belligerent submarines and aircraft from entering American territory; (8) expulsion from American ports of belligerent ships used as a base for espionage; (9) barring from American waters of belligerent ships that violate or may violate neutrality laws or American statutory laws; (10) announcement by the United States at the outset of a war of its intention that belligerent merchant ships will be considered adjuncts of belligerent navies and subject to internment under international law if they remain in American waters longer than the time prescribed by such laws for belligerent war vessels; (11) forbidding of loans to belligerents; and (12) forbidding of American enlistments in foreign armies and warning of American citizens that they trade with belligerents at their own risk.[9]

Allen W. Dulles, the legal adviser to the American delegation of the Geneva Disarmament Conference, challenged Warren in the next issue of *Foreign Affairs*. In his article, "The Cost of Peace," Dulles accepted Warren's idea that in the past American neutrality had proved futile but attacked his conclusion that severe limitation on trade with belligerents would be effective. Dulles argued: "So long as we show any disposition to protect our foreign trade and our citizens, or to defend our manifold interests abroad, which are both material and sentimental, the outbreak of a major conflict will bring the United States face to face with the same problems we met in the past, both in the period of 1807 to 1812 and before we entered the World War." Dulles advocated "a policy which should include first of all the element of cooperation with other powers who have the same interest and ideals as ourselves in the maintenance of the peace and, if these efforts fail and the peace is broken, we should prepare ourselves for that course of conduct which holds out the best prospects of keeping us from being drawn into the war." If the United States extended no protection for American interests abroad, as Warren suggested, Dulles argued it would mean a policy of nonintercourse, which the American people would never accept. He believed that the United States should consult with other nations for the maintenance of peace, reserving full freedom of action if consultation failed, and under certain circumstances, the government should not adopt the same attitude toward both groups of belligerents when one was taking collective action against a treaty-breaking state.[10] In short, Dulles wanted the United States to continue to protect American economic interests and citizens abroad and to cooperate with collective action against an aggressor power. His suggestions for cooperation with collective security efforts were almost identical to the promise made by Davis in Geneva in May 1933.

The American minister in Switzerland, Hugh Wilson, agreed with Dulles that the Davis point of view was the better one. He wrote to Secretary Hull in March 1934, "I do not look upon Mr. Davis' declaration as essentially a means to help the solution of the European problem, although it does help, but as essentially a means of limiting the risk of being drawn in if Europe goes into war."[11] Both Wilson and Davis looked upon the Geneva offer as the best means of defining American neutrality rights and avoiding involvement in another European war.

Despite the criticism of Dulles and others, certain department officials demonstrated a keen interest in Warren's position, particularly Moffat and R. Walton Moore. These two men lost patience with the international approach to the problem of peace and embraced the extreme isolationist policy Warren sponsored.[12] On April 17, 1934, Secretary Hull asked Legal Adviser Green Hackworth, Moffat, and Phillips to study neutrality with a view to keeping the United States out of war.[13] These department officials, busy with other problems, decided on June 1 to ask Warren to undertake a study on neutrality policy, working outside the department but with the cooperation of the State and Navy departments.[14] Warren agreed.

Warren submitted a long memorandum in August 1934, presenting in detail the program he had outlined in his article. One of his most important points called for the application of an impartial arms embargo when foreign wars broke out. He also suggested that arms shipments to other neutrals in wartime be limited to prewar levels to prevent the transshipment of war materiel to belligerents. A new idea—limiting all trade with belligerents to the prewar average—marked a radical departure from tradition. Warren argued: "Under modern conditions there is no reason why the United States Government should run the risk of becoming involved in a war simply to preserve such excessive profits to be made out of war-trading by some of its citizens."[15]

Otherwise his recommendations were the same ones he had presented in his article.

The State Department sent Warren's report to Roosevelt. The president expressed interest in the proposals, and he asked Hull to have the department prepare draft legislation. A neutrality committee was formed within the department, composed of Phillips, Moffat, Hackworth, and Moore. They accepted most of the points in Warren's memorandum, and the legal adviser was asked to prepare the actual draft. Some officials, including Phillips, hoped the legislation as finally conceived would grant permissive authority to the president rather than prescribe laws to govern fixed situations.[16] Accordingly, Hackworth's draft included most of Warren's suggestions but provided for presidential discretion. It omitted the suggestion that quotas be established on contraband material other than arms.

After approving Hackworth's draft, the State Department presented it to the Justice, War, and Navy departments. Justice and War accepted the draft legislation. The Navy Department dissented; it wanted no new rules governing neutrality.[17] Without the unanimous support of his executive departments, Roosevelt hesitated to recommend the legislation to Congress.

Not all members of the State Department endorsed the proposed neutrality bill. Moffat, in a conversation with the Swedish minister, "made it clear that our predominant purpose in studying a revision of our neutrality laws and policies was internal and motivated by our desire to assure ourselves of keeping out of any future war."[18] Davis, on the other hand, found the provision requiring the president to embargo arms to both belligerents contrary to his offer made in Geneva. He felt that while the disarmament conference was still technically alive, it would not be wise to inject a new American position on neutrality into the proceedings.[19] Secretary Hull, apparently convinced by Davis, spoke out in favor of the Geneva promise. Although he did not attack the neutrality bill, Hull proposed in a speech before the Canadian Society of New York that the United States not interfere with collective action against an aggressor.[20] Because of the division of opinion within the State Department, the departmental neutrality committee urged that action be withheld until it restudied the matter.

While the State Department dallied with its draft proposal, the Nye committee and publicists helped to crystallize public opinion in favor of a national approach to the neutrality question. During the fall of 1934, the Nye committee exposed many startling facts about the practices of the munitions industry. It uncovered the close connection between the munitions industry and the War and Navy departments, discovered extensive lobbying by the munitions makers in favor of military and navy appropriation bills, and proved that the armaments industry depended on foreign wars for prosperity and that the industry had accumulated huge profits during World War I. Newspapers publicized the hearings, and Nye used the press as a sounding board for his accusations. By the spring of 1935, the American public was convinced that the munitions makers helped to promote war.

Public opinion was also influenced in favor of neutrality legislation by the publication of Walter Millis's book, *Road to War: America, 1914–1917,* a Book-of-the-Month Club selection which sold widely. Millis presented a revisionist account of America's entry into World War I, charging that the country was duped by British propaganda, misled with respect to neutrality rights, and economically allied with the Entente before entering the war. His most telling observation dealt with neutrality. He demonstrated how the United States, by allowing British interference in American trade with Germany, had become an informal ally of the Entente. Millis concluded that the United States might have avoided involvement and adverse domestic consequences if an arms embargo had been applied early in the war. "The embargo would not have been the body blow either to American prosperity or the Allied war effort which it would have been later on. The export of raw materials and commercial supplies would have supported all the prosperity we needed; the Allies would have been driven sooner to organize their own munitions manufacture, as the Germans did, and the net result might well have been far more satisfactory to them as well as to the United States."[21]

By 1935 the American public was both excited with the Nye investigation and concerned with the developing European crisis. Germany had withdrawn from the Geneva Disarmament Conference, and in March Hitler started a rearmament program. Italy was already engaged in sporadic fighting in Ethiopia, and that conflict showed signs of ripening into war. The combination of internal and external pressures convinced the American public that the United States must not be drawn into another war, and neutrality legislation emerged as an important issue. The State Department still suffered from internal disagreements. Without clear-cut guidance from the department, Roosevelt delayed making any recommendations to Congress. But Senator Nye had aroused the public to such an extent that Congress had to take action.

Departmental sentiment was to continue international disarmament efforts by having the Senate ratify the 1925 Geneva Arms Convention or negotiate a new treaty. In February, Joseph C. Green asked Senator Nye to introduce a munitions control bill enabling the government to license and supervise the export of arms and munitions. Nye agreed but expressed a desire for legislation to abolish private munitions production and establish a government monopoly.[22] On March 14, 1935, Secretary Hull repeated Green's suggestion and commented upon the Nye proposal in a memorandum to Roosevelt: "It may be pointed out that the institution of a Government monopoly would seriously dislocate our whole economic structure, would curtail or put an end to several hundred private companies, and would put this Government in business to an extent unknown anywhere else in the world except in the U.S.S.R."[23] Green's remarks and Hull's memorandum show that the department preferred an international solution to the armaments question. Nye's proposal, which appeared socialistic to Hull and others, went beyond the economic thinking of the State Department, which preferred to maintain and promote capitalism by commercial expansion.

Roosevelt ignored Hull's memorandum. He met with the Nye committee on March 19, turned to the question of neutrality legislation, and asked the committee to study the problem and prepare a bill. Naturally, the State Department was dismayed by Roosevelt's decision. Phillips recorded in his diary: "The whole subject is a mess. When the President received the Nye Committee about ten days or two weeks ago he advised them to study the subject and introduce legislation looking to neutrality. Of course, the Nye Committee knew nothing about the subject whatsoever, now they are giving out long accounts in the papers as to what they propose to do. Our draft legislation was completed some time ago."[24] The department had to regroup if it was to have any voice in the neutrality issue.

On April 2, 1935, Hackworth presented a draft on neutrality legislation which resembled the one he had submitted in the fall of 1934. His proposal called for an embargo on arms and munitions to belligerents designated by the president, a prohibition against American ships carrying arms and munitions, the forbidding of the use of American ports as a base of supplies by belligerents, a declaration against submarines entering American waters, and a travel ban against American citizens using belligerent ships.[25] The department used Hackworth's draft as the basis for a memorandum it planned to submit to Roosevelt on April 10, stressing the need to "lessen the chances of being drawn into any future war."[26] Green raised strong objections to Hackworth's ideas, and Hull decided not to send the memorandum but instead to present the department's position in person, explaining the lack of agreement.[27] After meeting with the president, Hull had a press conference and stated that the department was still studying the neutrality question.[28] On the following day, Hull sent Roosevelt a memorandum reviewing the Nye committee's action and emphasizing the diversity of opinion on the issue. He offered to submit the Hackworth draft for

Roosevelt's consideration "although I am not prepared to advocate this or any other specific program for legislation on this subject at this time."[29] Hull's reluctance to endorse the department's draft legislation reflected his desire not to take sides on an issue on which his subordinates were divided.

While the State Department attempted to delay action on neutrality legislation, Congress put increasing pressure on the administration for the enactment of a law. On April 9, 1935, Senators Nye and Bennett Champ Clark introduced two neutrality resolutions. One resolution granted the president power to impose a travel ban; the other proposed that the floating of loans or extension of credit to belligerents be forbidden.[30] In the House, two congressmen introduced sweeping neutrality bills. Representative Maury Maverick of Texas introduced a resolution which included an embargo on arms and war materiel to all belligerents as well as a travel ban. Representative Frank L. Kloeb of Ohio introduced a bill prohibiting loans to belligerents.[31] Pressure from Maverick, who spoke in behalf of his resolution, along with the lobbying of the peace societies forced the House Foreign Affairs Committee to hold hearings on the Kloeb and Maverick bills in mid-June.[32]

On May 7, Senators Nye and Clark introduced a third resolution, which called for an embargo on the shipment of arms to all belligerents and stated that the government would not protect the export of goods declared contraband by belligerents and that such shipments would be at the risk of the exporter.[33] Introduction of these bills and the hearings in June further stimulated the national demand for neutrality legislation.

In the spring of 1935, the State Department renewed its effort to achieve an international control of the arms trade. Here the department achieved some success. Hull campaigned for unqualified Senate ratification of the 1925 Geneva Arms Convention, and on June 6 Senator Key Pittman brought the treaty before the Senate for approval. The Senate ratified the document,[34] finally giving the State Department support for its approach to the arms traffic problem. This success, however, was soon overshadowed by other developments. Without warning, the Senate Foreign Relations Committee reported out the Nye-Clark resolution providing for an impartial embargo on arms. When Hull learned of this development, he sent Norman H. Davis to persuade Senator Pittman to have the Senate committee reconsider its action. Davis seemed to have convinced Pittman to blunt the effect upon the Senate of the committee's decision, but as an additional precaution, he suggested that both Roosevelt and Hull meet with Pittman personally.[35] When Roosevelt did meet with Pittman on June 29, the president could not convince the senator to drop the impartial embargo approach.

The confusion surrounding the neutrality question led the House Foreign Affairs Committee to assume the administration was no longer interested in it and to report out the Kloeb bill banning loans to belligerents. Hull immediately secured a promise from Congressman McReynolds that he would prevent any neutrality bills from coming to a vote in the House. Hull then conferred with Pittman on July 8 and effected a compromise whereby the secretary could attend the next meeting of the Senate Foreign Relations Committee scheduled for July 10 so he could ask that the Nye-Clark bills be recalled for further study.[36]

Hull and Moore attended the Senate Foreign Relations Committee meeting. The secretary made some general comments about the complexity of the neutrality issue and stressed the need for careful study. Moore, however, antagonized the committee by presenting a detailed critique of the Nye-Clark resolutions. Yet the committee finally agreed to recall the resolutions and to appoint a subcommittee to work with the State Department in drafting neutrality legislation.[37] The State Department welcomed cooperation from the Senate subcommittee, but under no circumstances did it want to jeopardize disarmament efforts and the international arms traffic convention.[38] The central issue before the department was not simply whether to allow for a discriminatory embargo, as one historian argues, but whether the enactment of neutrality legislation would promote or impede European disarmament.[39]

Despite disagreements within the State Department, it continued to promote neutrality legislation that would keep the United States out of war but would not compromise the Geneva pledge. Congress also continued to obstruct the department's efforts. Therefore, the department attempted to convince members of Congress that legislation must not require the president automatically to execute neutrality provisions when war broke out or to invoke an arms embargo on all belligerents at the outbreak of war.[40]

Although meetings between the department and the Senate subcommittee on neutrality legislation continued until August 7, the subcommittee rejected the State Department's proposals and expressed its intention to recommend rigid neutrality legislation to the Foreign Relations Committee. The subcommittee prepared its own neutrality draft, which combined the State Department's proposals with the mandatory features of the Nye-Clark resolutions. The bill was rigid, proposing an impartial arms embargo, a travel ban, and an automatic prohibition against loans to belligerents. When the subcommittee presented its draft, the full committee split between advocates of rigid and flexible neutrality. Unable to reconcile these conflicting viewpoints, the committee instructed the subcommittee to formulate a compromise bill and report back on August 21.

While the Senate Foreign Relations Committee struggled with neutrality proposals, certain members of the State Department were voicing strong opposition to the entire concept of neutrality. Hornbeck expressed a minority opinion: "Not infrequently war is brought about by the definite intention of some nation to embark upon a predatory course. In such cases, there is nothing that could be settled by so-called 'peaceful or pacific processes.' The only thing that will deter the would-be aggressor is a threat of or introduction of force from without."[41] Hornbeck later asserted more firmly that in "any war which may occur, it may be definitely to our advantage that one side rather than the other win, and definitely to our disadvantage if the outcome be otherwise." Yet even Hornbeck recommended that if neutrality legislation were adopted, the bill should provide for presidential discretion because "the conducting of foreign relations is, under the Constitution, a function and the duty of the Chief Executive."[42]

By mid-August there seemed to be no chance for the enactment of neutrality legislation. But Senator Nye and the supporters of a rigid neutrality bill prepared for one last stand. The neutrality bloc in the Senate planned to filibuster, threatening important domestic legislation until the Senate acted upon neutrality. Roosevelt had indicated to one department official in July that nothing was to interfere with his domestic program.[43]

Senator Pittman contributed to the neutrality crusade by introducing a comprehensive bill with an impartial arms embargo. When the State Department learned of this maneuver, it sought the aid of the House and asked Representative McReynolds to sponsor the department's legislative proposal. On August 17, McReynolds agreed and introduced a bill with a flexible program including a discriminatory arms embargo and presidential authority to prohibit loans to belligerents. McReynolds's cooperation was limited. He issued a public statement that his measure represented the administration's position on neutrality and that he would not fight for its adoption until the next session of Congress.[44]

The situation became further complicated by indications that war was imminent between Italy and Ethiopia. Nye and Clark capitalized on the events in Africa to urge the Senate to act immediately on neutrality to prevent American involvement. In response, the department decided to make one last attempt to head off the Senate bill. On August 19, Norman Davis asked Green to prepare letters for the president requesting a new bill with presidential authority to embargo arms to any nation he selected in the event of war between Italy and Ethiopia.[45] Hull took these letters to Roosevelt, who signed them. But the president withdrew the letters when he learned that Pittman was not sympathetic to the department's latest recommendation.[46]

On August 20, Senator Homer T. Bone of Washington demanded immediate consideration of neutrality legislation. He was joined by Senators Clark and Nye, and this group began a filibuster. When it had been in progress for less than three hours, Pittman arrived with the Foreign Relations Committee's neutrality bill prepared three days previously. The draft recommended an impartial arms embargo, a prohibition against the use of American ships to transport munitions, and a travel ban. Pittman asked his colleagues to examine the measure overnight so that they could reach a decision the following day.[47] At that time, Pittman asked for and received unanimous support for the bill.

Once again, the department attempted to use its influence in the House to reverse the Senate's action. It decided to ask Roosevelt to persuade Representative McReynolds to kill the bill in the House. Roosevelt refused.[48] Instead, the president wrote to McReynolds that he would accept the Pittman bill if the arms embargo were limited to six months. On August 22, the House Foreign Affairs Committee met to review the Pittman resolution. Pittman, after conference with Roosevelt, attended the House Committee meeting and announced that the president had sent him to help with the redrafting of the resolution. At the committee meeting, the senator objected to all proposed amendments except the time limitation suggested by Roosevelt. Ultimately, the House committee acquiesced and agreed to report out the bill with the six-months limit. The next day the House passed the compromise bill, and on August 24 the Senate accepted the House amendments. Roosevelt signed the neutrality act on August 31. The department had lost its battle for a neutrality bill with presidential discretion.

On October 1, several members of the department met with Charles Warren in Hull's office. Phillips described the meeting in his diary:

> [Warren] recommends, and I think we all in the Department agree, that an embargo on the export of arms and

ammunition should be made to apply to both parties to the dispute, but that there should be nothing automatic about applying them. In other words, the President should be given freedom of decision as to whether to apply the embargo or not. . . . Warren thinks we should go further in neutrality legislation in giving the President powers to exclude armed merchant vessels from our ports. He thinks, however, this should not be mandatory, but permissive legislation.[49]

Hull concurred with the view of most of his subordinates. In a radio address on November 6, 1935, he stated that if arms embargo legislation were enacted, "the Executive should not be unduly or unreasonably handicapped."[50] To a man, the department's main objection to the neutrality bill was its rigidity, which precluded executive discretion.

The State Department's reaction to neutrality legislation was governed by the same set of assumptions that prompted its response to the arms embargo bill of 1933. Its main concern was the promotion of European peace based upon an international disarmament agreement. To effect this agreement, the department allowed Davis to offer an assurance at the Geneva conference that the United States would not interfere with collective efforts against an aggressor power by exercising its traditional neutrality rights, if the United States government agreed upon the designation of the guilty party and if disarmament had been effected beforehand. The promise made at Geneva in May 1933, coupled with the department officials' sincere desire to secure disarmament, prompted them to support a neutrality bill that would not cancel the Geneva pledge. Therefore, disagreement in the department did not involve the principle of insulating the United States from future wars. It centered upon certain provisions of the bill which either robbed the president and the State Department of control in a vital aspect of foreign policy or threatened to upset disarmament efforts.

The neutrality bill represented a significant departure from the principle of isolationism. That principle, announced by George Washington in his Farewell Address and followed for more than a century, emphasized avoiding entanglements in European politics. Above all, it provided for flexibility in American relations with European states. The department knew that the neutrality bill robbed the government of its freedom of action in European matters. As Herbert Feis recalls, "The Secretary of State and some of his staff smouldered with doubt in regard to what was underway. But this was permitted to appear only as a faint glow."[51] In this instance, the department might have followed the example of Hornbeck, who let his opposition to the bill burn more brightly.

7. Neutrality and the Italian - Ethiopian War

State Department handling of the Italian-Ethiopian war demonstrated its view of neutrality policy as a means to avoid political involvement in European problems. Although several officials in the department objected to the government's neutrality policy as applied to this war and believed the United States should help punish the aggressor, they remained silent out of fear of being proven wrong. The majority of department officers favored noninvolvement and denegated policies that might lead to a European war with American participation.[1]

As events developed, four closely related issues confronted the State Department: first, the timing of the neutrality proclamation; second, the general problem of trading with the belligerents and the specific problem of extending the contraband list to curtail excessive exports of war materiel; third, the question of cooperating with the League of Nations in imposing sanctions against Italy; and fourth, the decision, when hostilities ended, about recognizing the new order in Ethiopia. On each of these issues disagreement arose, yet the final decision in each instance sought to prevent American involvement.

The first issue, the timing of the neutrality proclamation, engendered considerable debate among department members. For a variety of reasons, some officials wanted the government to announce the neutrality proclamation immediately while others favored delay. On October 5, 1935, two days after Italy's invasion of Ethiopia, Minister Hugh Wilson telephoned from Geneva informing Hull that the League Council would probably not reach a decision on the existence of a state of war until the seventh.[2] Wilson later wrote and advised that "unless there are reasons to the contrary of which I am unaware you may think it advisable to delay action until the League has taken a position or at least until we ascertain more accurately which way the States over here are going to jump."[3] He also pointed out that if the United States took the first step in recognizing a state of war, it " 'would be a blow to the collective system which Geneva is trying to put through.' "[4]

In Washington, some officials, most vociferously Hornbeck and Phillips, had already indicated that they preferred to delay taking a stand. Hornbeck believed that the circumstances were such that the United States could "afford to wait a little while." Phillips's primary concern was that the United States might be "going out on a limb" by enacting the sanctions applicable to both parties under the neutrality act before other states made a decision.[5]

Other officials supported the immediate issuance of the neutrality proclamation for a variety of reasons. R. Walton Moore wanted the announcement made right away because he feared congressional reaction to a dilatory policy. Joseph Green urged speed to avoid criticism from Roosevelt. Before leaving Washington for a vacation in September, the president had signed a neutrality proclamation for Hull to release if war broke out between Italy and Ethiopia during his absence. Roosevelt wired Hull on October 4 stating that any battle reports from Ethiopia would necessitate a proclamation of American neutrality even though war had not actually been declared.[6] Breckinridge Long, the American ambassador to Italy, wanted an immediate announcement to avoid Italian speculation that the United States might join collective efforts to punish aggression. Long's opinion apparently carried considerable weight with the president. When Roosevelt instructed Hull on October 5 to announce American neutrality, he said, "I agree with Ambassador Long that our neutrality declaration should be issued before action by the League."[7]

Secretary Hull concurred. Certain that the League would be forced to recognize the hostilities, he believed the United States would have to apply at least the arms embargo portion of the neutrality act, and he wanted to do so before the League took action. Consequently, on the same day he received Roosevelt's instructions, Hull wired the president that he thought the department had sufficient evidence of war to justify the announcement.[8]

The State Department divided about equally on the question of the timing of the neutrality proclamation. Within the department, Hull made the decision to support an announcement before the League of Nations acted. Hull listened to those advisers who advocated an immediate announcement because he wanted to avoid creating the impression that the United States was involved in collective efforts to restore peace in Ethiopia. The decision would represent an important precedent in its effect on future cases involving neutrality by demonstrating that any advice for bold action or for cooperation with the League, which embroiled the United States in European politics, would go unheeded.

A second issue confronting the State Department involved trade with the belligerents, especially in commodities other than arms. Under the provisions of the neutrality act, the government could prevent the shipment of arms and ammunition to nations at war, although it could not legally stop the exportation of other war materiel. Therefore, to implement the spirit as well as the letter of the neutrality law, the State Department turned its attention to avoiding trade with the belligerents. Once again, department opinion split, some advocating moral appeals or stronger methods to curtail trade, others objecting to any restraints on commercial contact with the warring states.

Roosevelt wired Hull on October 4 requesting that the department consider issuing a statement to accompany the declaration of neutrality that would indicate the administration's intention to publish the names of all Americans traveling on Italian ships and make public the cargo lists of all American goods sent to either belligerent, including the export of raw materials.[9] Hull believed that such a statement was too drastic, and he suggested an alternative accompanying statement: "In order that our country may by no possibility be involved . . . I desire it to be understood that any of our people who voluntarily engage in transactions of any character with either of the belligerents do so at their own risk." Should circumstances so warrant, he added that Roosevelt might wish to take the following successive steps: first, an appeal; second, a warning if the appeal were ignored; and third, the publication of the names of uncooperative citizens.[10]

Department opinion diverged concerning the efficacy of the accompanying statement. Feis, the staunchest supporter of the collateral announcement, wrote a memorandum in its defense, in which he presented eight elements to consider in the preparation of the statement: (1) the action would aid in preventing American involvement with the belligerents; (2) Italy would be affected more than Ethiopia; (3) despite some loss of trade, economic considerations were secondary; (4) action taken before any action by the League would encourage sanctions; (5) an indication of the American position with regard to trade would clear any doubts among League powers as to the government's attitude, although there had been repeated expressions of the intention to keep out of the war; (6) American public opinion would regard an independent announcement before League action as an expression of the desire to avoid the war (by demonstrating the wish not to interfere with international peace machinery and representing an effort to avoid disagreement with League members should the United States continue normal trade relations with Italy in the face of widespread sanctions); (7) proposals for ceasing shipments to Italy would be more plainly understood as a desire to avoid entanglements than proposals for ceasing purchases, which Italy would interpret as a sanction; and (8) whatever was done would establish a precedent.[11]

William Phillips was among the department officials who advised against issuing the accompanying statement. He noted in his diary:

I do not think any of us approved the step, but there was nothing to be done about it. Personally I felt that this was going beyond the state of neutrality and was, in fact, a sanction against Italy because it was a warning to Americans to avoid the southern route during the winter months and might mean a discontinuance of travel on the Italian route and so affect disastrously the SS REX and other passenger vessels, while of course, Ethiopia would be unaffected.[12]

Assistant Secretary Moore shared Phillips's view, and he warned that steps to discourage trade would be viewed by the Congress as an unwarranted interference designed to hurt Italy.[13]

Roosevelt directed Hull to issue a statement warning Americans against travel on belligerent ships and adopted the secretary's suggestion to limit trade restrictions to a simple warning without the threat of publicity. As finally conceived, the plan to release an additional announcement did not, as Divine argues it did, represent "a novel attempt to transcend the inflexible limitations of the 1935 neutrality act."[14] For Secretary Hull argued, "The warning given by the President in his proclamation concerning travel on belligerent ships and his general warning that during the war any of our people who voluntarily engage in transactions of any character with either of the belligerents do so at their own risk were based upon the policy and purpose of keeping this country out of war—keeping it from being drawn into war."[15] Although some department officials were distressed by this limited statement, and there was general disagreement over the wisdom of issuing the warning, both the supporters and critics agreed that the United States must avoid involvement. The argument centered upon tactics and not upon overall neutrality policy.

Another trade problem the department faced concerned extending the embargo to include war materials other than arms or warning citizens that such trade violated the spirit of the neutrality proclamation. Some doubted the practicality of the presidential warning. An unsigned memorandum asserted that the statement would not restrict commerce with the belligerents in goods other than arms because "the profit motive will prove to be so strong that the trade will continue unless further discouraged." Consequently, the memorandum suggested a stronger statement or a broader definition of arms in the president's proclamation.[16] Both recommendations were given serious consideration in November 1935, and the latter generated debate within the State Department.

Somehow the press learned that the department wanted more stringent measures to curtail trade with the warring nations and speculated that the Roosevelt administration might extend the embargo. When Ambassador Long read these accounts, he concluded: "It would be a very dangerous thing to do as far as keeping us out of the conflict is concerned. My impression is that it would be a manifestation of un-neutrality rather than adherence to strict neutrality."[17] Nevertheless, the department gave serious thought to extending the embargo.

On November 12, 1935, a meeting was called to discuss the problem of discouraging shipments of war materiel. Department officials decided that rather than extend the embargo list, the president should issue another appeal requesting the public to refrain from exporting such products as oil, scrap iron, steel, tractors, and trucks to either of the belligerents and that such an appeal should be released before League sanctions went into effect to avoid the impression that the United States was following that organization's lead.[18] On November 15, Hull gave the department's statement to the press. It read as follows: "The American people are entitled to know that there are certain commodities, such as oil, copper, trucks, tractors, scrap iron and scrap steel, which are essentially war materials although not actually 'implements of war' and that, according to recent government trade reports, a considerably increased amount of these was being exported for war purposes."[19] As finally conceived, the statement was a gentle appeal to the public.

It further demonstrated that department decisions reflected a desire to avoid bold action that might be interpreted as a sanction against Italy or an indication of cooperation with the League.[20]

Phillips regarded the statement as an important step because it preceded League sanctions and served notice that the U.S. government intended to pursue an independent policy. Even Ambassador Long responded favorably. He feared that "if the United States Government had placed an embargo on oil it would have made [it] possible for Geneva to close the ring and would have precipitated the European war."[21]

The State Department's attitude toward commercial intercourse with the belligerents raised a fundamental question with respect to neutrality. Would the department recommend that the government insist upon its rights as a neutral, or would the department follow the ideas of Warren and limit contact with the belligerents to avoid involvement, though to do so meant surrendering traditional rights under international law? Department sentiment was split. Phillips and Long subscribed to the former idea; they insisted upon America's right to trade. Feis and Hull subscribed to the latter idea; they wanted the United States to modify its stand on neutral rights to prevent embroilment in the war. On one issue sentiment was unanimous—whatever policy the government pursued concerning trade, the end result must be noninvolvement.

The question of cooperating with League powers in the application of sanctions against Italy for aggression in Ethiopia was a third major issue facing the State Department. Again, one group endorsed and another rejected cooperation. The American ambassador in Italy supported a policy of appeasement. One official who favored cooperation in the early stages of the Italo-Ethiopian conflict changed his mind once the fighting actually began. Finally, the department refused all invitations for collective action.

Before the outbreak of hostilities, Davis and Hornbeck advised working with the League. Davis wanted the govern-

ment to use a variation of his Geneva formula, making it
clear that, if other nations agreed that Italy was responsible
for war in Ethiopia and the United States concurred, the
government should not adopt a policy that would interfere
with collective efforts to punish the wrongdoer.[22] Hornbeck
endorsed cooperation, noting that "a breach or a threatened
breach of the peace is a matter of rightful and of inevitable
concern to every member of the community to endeavor to
prevent breaches of the peace." Hornbeck later recommended that the United States express publicly its moral
support for the efforts of League powers in the Ethiopian
controversy because League sanctions would be ineffective if
the United States refused to comply.[23] And the chief of the
Far Eastern Division saw it as a way "to demonstrate our
whole-hearted interest in the League as part of the world's
'peace machinery.' "[24]

Not everyone in the department shared the views of Davis
and Hornbeck. Ambassador Long rejected the idea of working with the League. Long's attraction to fascism undoubtedly clouded his judgment. As early as August 1933, he
wrote to a friend that Italy was "the scene of the most interesting experiment in political science which has evolved
since our Government was formed under the Constitution. . . . The outstanding fact is that they are doing it here
. . . under the guidance of [a] remarkable man. Incidentally,
he is one of the most interesting personalities I have come
in contact with through a long period of experience." Long
thought the fascist powers, Italy and Germany, provided a
bulwark against the spread of Bolshevism and would protect
European civilization. He reasoned that if Germany and Italy win a war, "domination would be accompanied by an
autocratic but enlightened spread of culture followed by an
increase of commerce and a revival of industry."[25]

In September 1935, Long submitted to the department a
"compromise" solution to the Italian-Ethiopian conflict that
essentially called for the total capitulation of Ethiopia. He
argued that the conflict was beyond the League's jurisdic-
tion. His plan "would give Italy, but without war, the low-

lands of Abyssinia, joining the two Italian colonies, and the uplands, including Adis Ababa. . . . It is probably not acceptable to Italy. . . . Probably no solution is, but I am satisfied that that is the basis upon which agreements must be made if peace is to be maintained in Europe." Subsequently, Long sent a telegram in which he expressed his opposition to joining the League of Nations in imposing sanctions against Italy. As he noted in his diary, "I advised that the American Government act under the terms of that [neutrality] law without reference to any other Government and that its actions be so timed and so explained that it would exclude the inference that it was acting in concert with other Powers."[26] In all probability, the ambassador made the recommendation with Italian interests in mind.

Other members of the State Department opposed cooperation with the League for different reasons. Hull, for instance, had faith in the Kellogg Pact. He remarked, "We have signed, along with sixty-two other nations, including Italy and Ethiopia, a treaty in which the signatories have condemned war as a instrument of national policy and have undertaken, each to all, to settle their disputes by none but pacific means." Beyond that expression of faith and a call for Italy and Ethiopia to live up to the treaty, Hull would not go. At the end of September, he made it clear in his instructions to the American chargé in Great Britain that this government would not join in the imposition of sanctions upon any nation involved in the pending controversy.[27] Hull's main concern was to avoid the impression that the United States would follow the League. He did not want the country to become immersed in any collectivist schemes.

After hostilities actually began in Ethiopia, department opinion largely united behind a policy of noncooperation. Only a minority still wanted the United States to work with the League. The shift in Hornbeck's position was indicative of the growing consensus. Before the war began, he had spoken out for cooperation. Once fighting started, he discouraged that policy. On October 4, the day after Italy invaded Ethiopia, Hornbeck submitted a memorandum that contradicted a recommendation he had made six days earlier. Hornbeck's suggestion that the British be discouraged from inviting American participation in the use of sanctions "was greeted with smiles of disapproval."[28] Hornbeck might have misinterpreted the smiles. The amused response of his colleagues may have been prompted by the rapidity of his change of heart, for, a short time later, the department adopted the very same suggestion he offered in the October 4 memorandum.

On October 9, Wilson, the American minister in Geneva, sent a telegram to the department intimating that the United States would receive an invitation to work with the League's Committee of Coordination on the question of sanctions. He presented arguments for and against participation, but officials in Washington felt that involvement would be highly undesirable.[29] Wilson was told to inform the League that "it would seem unnecessary and certainly at the present stage inadvisable from our point of view to ask us to participate in such committee as may be set up to deal with sanctions."[30] Several officials in the department agreed with the instructions. Phillips, in particular, regarded the reply to Wilson as an excellent statement of the American position and sincerely hoped it precluded any future invitations from the League.[31]

Despite the announced position of the American government, European newspapers circulated the rumor that the United States intended to participate in international efforts to apply sanctions. To counteract the rumors, the State Department instructed the American consul in Geneva to explain American policy, emphasizing the intention of the government to follow an independent policy. Shortly thereafter, the State Department drafted an official response to the League's inquiry. On October 26, Hull served notice that "the course thus pursued in advance of action by other governments ... represents the independent and affirmative policy of the Government of the United States and indicates its purpose not to contribute to a prolongation of the war."[32] The League, however, was not discouraged. Invitations for American participation continued.

Within the department the reaction to the secretary's declaration to the League varied. Phillips apparently underwent a change of heart and noted in his diary that the response "was as tough a document as I have ever had anything to do with . . . because we are so hampered by the Act of Congress providing strict neutrality." Long, on the other hand, was gratified by the stern reply: "Hull made an excellent reply to the League of Nations enquiry as to the American stand on sanctions. . . . [And] it will be very practical as far as we are concerned if it carries out what I hope will be the policy of the United States to stay strictly out of this war."[33] Regardless of the mixed response among department officials, policy crystallized by the end of October. Added to the doctrine of noninvolvement was the doctrine of noncooperation.

The response to Ethiopian inquiries about American policy also demonstrated the State Department's intention to follow an independent course of action. At the end of October, the American chargé in Ethiopia, C. Van H. Engert, asked whether he was interpreting government policy correctly:

> I am often asked how it is that in 1933 the United States expressed readiness not to interfere with any collective pressure that might be adopted against an aggressor state, while now our neutrality laws and arms embargo make no distinction between the aggressor and the victim. My reply is that our attitude in 1933 had been expressly contingent upon the signing of a general disarmament agreement and that when no such agreement was reached we retained complete freedom of action. Am I correct?[34]

Hull referred Engert to the text of his October 26 reply to the League's Committee of Coordination and sent him a text of Davis's Geneva pledge.[35] Together the two documents answered Engert's question—the United States had an independent policy, and its Geneva pledge, predicated upon substantial European disarmament, was no longer valid. If the State Department harbored any sympathy for Ethiopia, that sympathy never materialized in the department's policy.

During November, reports reached the State Department that the subcommittee of the League's Coordination Committee was considering a commodity embargo against Italy including such products as coal, iron, steel, and oil and intended to request U.S. cooperation. Phillips, then acting secretary of state, instructed Wilson to say that "in the face of the independent actions of this Government you do not believe that anyone would wish to precipitate a controversy over here and inject confusion into the situation by querying us with regard to any action we might take with respect to any particular commodity in connection with the program under discussion or contemplated by the states members of the League."[36] Although Hull made a public statement discouraging commodity shipments to belligerents two weeks after the League put out these feelers, his announcement represented an independent step before the League acted to avoid the impression that the United States was cooperating with international sanctions against Italy.

Of commodities shipped to Italy, oil was the most vital. Certain department members such as Feis wanted an oil embargo to supplement League sanctions, for, as he observed, "the growth of American sales of oil . . . gave genuine ground for the fear that a League ban could not work without participation by the United States." Phillips, however, feared that an oil embargo would leave the United States on a limb which the League could saw off by not adopting an embargo. Events justified his anxiety. At the end of November, the League postponed adding oil to its list of sanctions because Mussolini threatened war with those nations embargoing oil.[37]

Ambassador Long adamantly opposed even these limited steps to curtail oil exports. On November 12, he cabled the department reiterating his belief in strict neutrality and charging that the present policy toward Italy was not strictly neutral. He cautioned: "I believe the American policy, making possible [a] league embargo on oil for Italy, will force that Government to an early action and bring on a European war in the near future." Sensing that his views differed from the department's, Long decided to communicate directly with Roosevelt. He wrote to the president on November 29, arguing that an American oil embargo would bring the United States into the war:

I have telegraphed to the Department until I am blue in the face. I feel that they have resented some of my telegrams because they contained recommendations which seemed to be at variance with a policy which they had already adopted but which I had not been sufficiently advised about to understand properly.... The Department has made me feel that they resented the receipt of certain telegrams and they were displeased with advice which I feel it my right and duty to give.[38]

Long's estimation of the department's feeling was probably correct, for, shortly after the Italian-Ethiopian War ended, he was removed from his post. But his desire to stay out of the conflict and avoid cooperation with the League was shared by the bulk of the officials in Washington.

An additional indication of the department's desire to maintain an independent course was its response to continued overtures from League powers for the United States to join them in applying a commodity sanction. On December 5, for example, the British ambassador asked Hull if the United States would keep oil exports to Italy from exceeding normal levels should the League adopt an oil embargo. Hull replied negatively. He reviewed American policy, referred to American obligations under the Kellogg Pact, and noted that his own and the president's public statements made the government's position abundantly clear. In the future, the government "would continue to pursue its separate, independent course in dealing with all phases of the present war and would refrain from the slightest agreements or understanding with other nations or groups of nations in that connection."[39] Once again, the department turned down an invitation for collective action.

The advocates of cooperation within the department continued to look for ways the government might change its policy. At the end of December, Hackworth submitted a memorandum suggesting that "there is no reason why a neutral may not change its position with respect to exports as its interests may seem to require. This does not, of course, mean that if a belligerent is adversely affected it may not regard the action as unfriendly." Several days later Hornbeck criticized Hackworth's memorandum, but he also questioned the concept of neutrality policy: "It might be well for all nations to consider more seriously than any appear as yet to have done whether it is really desirable that there be "neutrals" and whether it is practicable for any country to expect that efforts on its part to follow a course of 'neutrality' will 'keep it out of war.' "[40]

In spite of intradepartmental disagreements, policy remained the same—noncooperation. Secretary Hull, at pains to distinguish American policy from the League's, argued: "The essential difference between sanctions and the policy followed by this Government is that the former seek to punish Italy and assist Ethiopia while this Government has sought, by strictly impartial measures, to avoid the possibility of becoming involved in the conflict."[41] The secretary accurately distinguished American policy from that of the League powers. Strict neutrality, motivated by a desire to prevent American involvement, was basically different from the collective action of European states. Noninvolvement and noncooperation provided the basis for departmental policy, and it remained unchanged throughout the war.

A fourth issue the department faced dealt with the question of recognizing Italian sovereignty in Ethiopia once the war ended and revoking the neutrality proclamation. Its reaction indicated there was no desire to withhold recognition or to continue the moral restrictions on trade as a sign of protest against the outcome of events. With one exception among its policy formulators, the State Department advised that recognition be extended and the proclamation revoked as soon as Italian dominance was substantiated.

After Italy completed its conquest in May 1936, various officials cautioned against extending immediate recognition. Hackworth admitted, "We shall probably be under the necessity of treating with Italy as the sovereign power in Ethiopia," but, he advised, "for the time being action by this Government should await further announcements on the part of Italy." Phillips made a similar suggestion and advised that the United States wait until other governments, presumably League powers, with more immediate interests in the area made their decision. Similarly, Hornbeck "believed that this Government should persevere in its attitude of 'watchful waiting' and should continue to take no action toward proclaiming, as for this country, that the 'state of war' between Italy and Ethiopia is at an end."[42]

Just before the revocation of the neutrality proclamation, the chargé in Ethiopia, Engert, reported that some fighting was still going on. Consequently, Hull advised Roosevelt not to revoke the neutrality proclamation until he reported further. Shortly thereafter, Hull decided that the occasional skirmishes between Italian and Ethiopian forces did not constitute war, and he communicated this sentiment to Engert. Engert disagreed and continued to urge that recognition be withheld. His advice was ignored. Hackworth submitted a memorandum in which he distinguished guerrilla warfare from war between sovereign states. He pointed out that the congressional neutrality resolution stipulated that guerrilla warfare was not a real war and that, therefore, the department had no choice.[43] Regardless of the departmental debate, Roosevelt decided to revoke the proclamation on June 20, 1936.[44] For all practical purposes the Ethiopian problem ended.

The Italian-Ethiopian conflict demonstrated the State Department's attitude toward the problem of collective efforts to maintain peace. When the war began, the department,

with only a few dissenting voices, did not want entanglements with what was considered an exclusively European
problem. The department timidly followed the letter of the
neutrality law and tried to disassociate American policy
from that of the League of Nations.

8. Beyond Neutrality to Noninterference: The Spanish Civil War

The Spanish civil war occupies a unique place in the history of the interwar years. It symbolized the ideological conflicts between fascism, communism, and liberal democracy. It was the *cause célèbre* of the 1930s; it made dispassionate policy making difficult. One historian observed, "There was something pure about the Spanish war. The enthusiasm it engendered was a springtime that briefly loosened the wintry grip of a world grown old and weary and cynical."[1] Disagreements within the State Department, by and large, resembled differences of opinion elsewhere. An influential group supported the rebel forces of General Francisco Franco while a less persuasive faction supported the Loyalist government in power.[2]

Despite internal dissension, at the outset of the war in 1936 the department officially advocated a policy of noninterference, which the administration implemented. This position was held for the duration of the conflict. In adopting noninterference, the department was in effect endorsing the efforts of Britain and France to limit the war to Spain and prevent it from escalating into a world war. The department did not, however, advocate joining the Nonintervention Committee, the formal expression of European attempts to localize the conflict. Rather, it advocated an independent policy paralleling the one pursued by European powers anxious to contain the fighting.[3]

Contrary to contemporary popular misconceptions, the Spanish struggle was not a war to save Catholicism, protect capitalism, or make Spain safe for democracy. The conflict represented a violent expression of century-old tensions. Since the Napoleonic era, Spain's growth was stunted by at least three quarrels: the church versus the liberals, the landowners and bourgeoisie versus the workers, and the advocates of local autonomy in Catalonia and the Basque provinces versus those supporting central control by Castile. Disputes were common and became increasingly violent, taking on religious, class, and regional characteristics. Historian Hugh Thomas explained the prevailing attitude:

> All Spaniards were . . . aware that Spain had once been the greatest nation in the world, that at that time the country had at least seemed to be united, and that these continual disputes were unworthy of so great a history. This partly at least caused Spaniards to think that there was something undignified in any compromise of their ideals.[4]

Events immediately preceding the civil war tell a pathetic tale of a quixotic nation tilting at a political windmill. Spain lagged behind the rest of Europe in political and social development. Changes in the climate of opinion swept in successive regimes. Following World War I, as a reaction to economic dislocations in Spain, King Alfonso XIII allowed a dictatorship under General Prime de Rivera. After initial successes, the government went into eclipse when de Rivera dispensed with the constitution, abolished free elections, curtailed freedom of speech, and rigidly controlled the press. Facing imminent revolution, the king dismissed de Rivera and appointed General Demaso Berenguer as premier. Berenguer stayed in office less than a year. He was succeeded by Admiral Don Juan B. Aznar, who endured an equally short time.

April 1931 marks the turning point in current Spanish history. In that month, republican-socialist parties triumphed in municipal elections. King Alfonso abdicated, and

Spain anticipated a new political millennium. The republic was proclaimed on April 12, 1931. In June, elections were held for the Constituent Cortes. But salvation did not come. There were no political messiahs in Spain. The country seethed with violence and unrest. Political parties represented every conceivable shade of conviction. On the right were Carlists (conservative monarchists), fascists, and a number of right-center groups. On the left, there were moderate socialists, radical socialists, syndicalists, anarcho-syndicalists, and anarchists. Spain certainly did not offer a case study in political stability or democratic institutions.

From 1931 to 1933 a left-wing government under Don Manuel Azana, predominantly socialist in orientation, led the country. His regime failed to maintain the support of either left or right. He alienated right-wing groups by attacking traditional church prerogatives and left-wing groups when he failed to inaugurate suitable agrarian reform. These internal tensions climaxed with the brutal suppression of a revolt in Gasas Viejas in January 1933. Municipal elections that year reflected a profound change in the popular temper. Conservatives won with impressive majorities. Therefore, in the autumn of 1933, Azana resigned and dissolved the Cortes.

General elections in November 1933 brought in a center-right government. The regime dedicated itself to undoing all the socialists' work. It concentrated on hampering left-wing legislation and making constitutional revisions impossible. Moreover, the government postponed secularization of education, restored the state-supported clergy, and inaugurated an agrarian law respectful to large landowners. In the tradition of Spanish politics, the center-right government rapidly lost popular favor, and, by the end of 1935, new elections were scheduled.

A left coalition government, the Frente Popular, won the 1936 election. President-elect Azana led a coalition of parties which included, in addition to his own, the republican left, republican union, socialists, communists, Trotskyists, syndicalists, and anarchists.[5] These parties had cooperated to win the election, but political divisions in the Cortes remained.

Soon after the new regime assumed office, Spain exploded in strikes, riots, shootings, and church desecrations. An anemic parliament and ineffectual government could do nothing to avoid the approaching crisis. Finally, when José Calvo Sotelo, a leader of the militant right, was assassinated in July 1936, the army used the event as an excuse for precipitating rebellion. Civil war was on.

Obviously, the Spanish civil war resulted from unstable political and social institutions. The army represented those seeking to preserve their traditional dominance, whereas the left wanted change, defined in as many different ways as there were parties. The internecine struggle that followed was less a conflict between democracy and fascism than the result of a chronic disease in the body politic.

European intervention in the Spanish war made that conflict a significant international issue. From the beginning, Germany and Italy shipped men and supplies to Franco, ultimately enabling him to win. France and Russia aided the Loyalists, but the help they gave was small and spasmodic in comparison to the Axis contribution to the rebels. Because of the official European nonintervention policy, Republican forces could not secure sufficient war materiel.[6]

A French note of August 8, 1936, together with replies from twenty-seven nations, comprised the nonintervention agreement. In September, a meeting was held and the full committee of twenty-seven members proved too unwieldy. Therefore, a subcommittee, consisting of Belgium, Britain, Czechoslovakia, France, Germany, Italy, Russia, and Sweden, was created. The smaller body carried out concrete plans to prevent men and munitions from reaching Spain. Individual contributions of the participating states financed its activities. Monetary difficulties hampered the committee's effectiveness, however, because many members were in arrears with their dues, an indication of the organization's lack of support. Britain and France eventually assumed the burden of supporting the body, a development that reflected their paramount interest in its success.[7]

Although France initiated the nonintervention agreement, Britain engineered that stratagem. Leon Blum, head of the Popular Front coalition in France, could not risk a fight with Germany and Italy in Spain. Some evidence suggests that his shaky government would have collapsed if war had occurred.[8] Without active British support, France remained helpless against the combined might of Germany and Italy. Britain, on the other hand, wanted to prevent the conflict from spreading, a policy supported by both Prime Minister Stanley Baldwin and Chancellor of the Exchequer Neville Chamberlain. When the Nonintervention Committee ceased to have any practical value, however, participation was of little advantage and no credit to the British government.[9]

The nonintervention system represented a departure from international law. Legally, during an insurrection, the established government could purchase supplies to suppress a revolt, foreign states might accord recognition of belligerency if hostilities reached the magnitude of war, and a hands-off policy was expected for the duration of the struggle.[10] Legality notwithstanding, the agreement failed to prevent intervention.[11] At one point, Franco's army contained sixty thousand Italians, fifteen thousand Moroccans, and only between fifteen and twenty thousand Spaniards, while the Republican forces were almost entirely Spanish except for between six and ten thousand foreigners.[12] Presumably fear made Britain, and, to a lesser extent, France, keep supporting the moribund nonintervention program.

The American reaction to developments in Spain involved three closely related questions: whether to participate in the nonintervention agreement; whether to participate in international mediation efforts to end the conflict; and how to prevent the shipment and transshipment of American arms and ammunition to Spain in the absence of covering legislation. Each of these issues, though treated separately here, was intertwined with the others.

By and large, policy makers in the department were in agreement during the Spanish civil war, though some writings by participants after the war present a different picture. Claude Bowers, American ambassador to Spain during the war, wrote: "I was entirely satisfied with my position throughout. I found there was a sharp division in the State Department on our policy in Spain, though the pro-Franco element was more numerous, and strategically placed. Mr. Messersmith, then an Assistant Secretary, was sympathetic toward my point of view, and he assured me that the same was true of Sumner Welles, the Undersecretary."[13] Bowers also contended: "Had the Spanish Republic, recognized by every democratic nation as the legal constitutional government, not been shamefully denied its right, under universally recognized international law, to buy arms and ammunition for its defense, the Loyalists would have prevailed."[14]

These statements give the false impression that at the time of the civil war Bowers had disapproved of the department's policy, which denied the Loyalists the opportunity to buy arms from the United States. During the first year of the war, however, Bowers wrote Hull, "I think we should continue our present policy without deviation. This is a serious European quarrel [with] which we have no proper part."[15] Similarly, after the civil war Sumner Welles wrote, "Of all our blind isolationist policies, the most disastrous was our attitude on the Spanish Civil War."[16] Yet, in 1936, he also had agreed with the policy laid down by the secretary of state.[17]

Of all the officials who wrote on American policy during the Spanish civil war, Hull was the most candid and accurate. He took issue with the critics of the government's policy:

> Looking back with keen hindsight, critics of our policy can say it was wrong because the fascist forces in Spain eventually triumphed, Hitler and Mussolini were strengthened, and Britain and France humbled. This argument would be valid only if the peace-loving nations, including the United States had been prepared militarily and psychologically to abandon their efforts toward maintaining peace and embark on a general preventive war. Such was not the case.

Hull contended that he and the president decided upon a policy of noninterference (a synonym for noninvolvement) for three reasons. First, because of the Nonintervention Committee backed by Britain and France, it would have been unthinkable for the United States to pursue a different course, since those states were more directly concerned with events in Spain. Second, the Nonintervention Committee aimed to prevent the escalation of the Spanish conflict into a general war, a policy approved by both the president and the secretary of state. Third, the war threatened American security. Shipments of war materiel to the Spanish government might have plunged the United States into war.[18] Thus in his memoirs Hull defended American policy, and his recollections accurately reflect his feelings in 1936. Post-mortem statements in the writings of other department officials notwithstanding, the State Department closed ranks behind the secretary's policy.

Hull determined the government's attitude toward the Spanish civil war.[19] When the war broke out in mid-July 1936, Roosevelt was cruising off the New England coast. Initial decision responsibility governing American policy fell upon the secretary's shoulders. Hull followed events in Europe closely and decided to pursue an independent policy but one which supplemented the policies of Britain and France. By the end of July, he already knew that a nonintervention agreement was in the works. Consequently, he felt compelled to declare the American position as soon as possible. On August 5, Hull called a meeting of his advisers to discuss a public statement of American policy. Phillips, Moore, Welles, Hackworth, and others attended the meeting. After extended discussion, the group decided to issue an announcement calling attention to the article of the Montevideo Convention which stipulated: "No state has the right to intervene in the internal or external affairs of another."[20] Although they also decided to postpone the announcement, the policy makers felt it necessary to inform department members in the field about the American position. On August 7, a circular telegram sent to all representatives in Spain stated, "this Government will, of course, scrupulously refrain from any interference whatsoever in the unfortunate Spanish situation. We believe that American citizens, both at home and abroad, are patriotically observing this well-recognized American policy."[21] The reference to the conduct of American citizens was an appeal to Americans to effect a voluntary embargo that the department hoped to establish in the absence of a law. Shortly thereafter the department released these instructions to the press. The circular telegram and the press release announcing the government's policy were referred to frequently by department members when foreign representatives inquired about the American stance, for these documents contained the two essential ingredients of American policy toward Spain— noninterference and a voluntary embargo.

Hornbeck objected to the public announcement. He observed:

> Whatever we do with regard to the conflict in Spain, we should refrain as far as possible from explanation of our action, in public statements or written communications which may be made regarding it, with any use of inexact legal terminology or with broad generalities in regard to policy such (either of which) as might be cited to our embarrassment in connection with other situations either actual or which may develop elsewhere in the future.[22]

But Hornbeck was ignored. Throughout the year, the State Department issued public statements and wrote communications using the broad generality—noninterference.

One of the major questions confronting the State Department involved participating in or cooperating with the Nonintervention Committee. For the first time, the department decided upon a course of action which, in effect, supported the collective efforts of European states. Ironically, in this instance cooperation meant noninvolvement, already one of the cardinal principles of the State Department's foreign policy. Yet at no time did the department entertain thoughts of actually participating in the Nonintervention Agreement.[23]

Before the department publicly announced its Spanish policy, informal statements were made to foreign representatives. For example, on August 4, the French *chargé-d'affaires* visited Hull, telling him that the French government had proposed to the British and Italian governments that each should remain aloof from the Spanish situation by maintaining an attitude of neutrality or nonintervention. Hull "remarked casually in closing that of course the Chargé was aware of the general attitude of this Government towards the doctrine of nonintervention."[24] Hull implied that the idea of nonintervention in the internal affairs of other states, already an integral part of American foreign relations, would be followed in the Spanish situation.

Hull reiterated this response on a subsequent occasion. When the State Department received reports that the French government might invite the United States to adhere to the proposed nonintervention pact, the French chargé was called in by the department. He denied the validity of such reports, but Acting Secretary of State Phillips felt compelled to restate the American position and read the French representative a copy of the department's circular telegram of August 7.[25]

In December, Britain and France asked the State Department to state publicly its moral support for the Nonintervention Committee and a mediation scheme worked out by those two states. Moore, then acting secretary of state, wired Hull the following recommendation:

> I feel that we could very properly give renewed expression at this time to the position we have maintained since the beginning of the conflict in Spain, that is, of noninterference in the Spanish situation, and that we might very well also express a hope that some way might be found to relieve the human suffering result-

ing from the strife. I have even thought that it would be entirely appropriate for the President if he felt like so doing to make a general statement which while entirely independent of the steps taken by the British and French would be helpful in support of their most laudable effort.[26]

Ultimately, the department issued a statement offering moral support for the British and French efforts, but the expression did not represent any deviation in policy.[27] The United States never joined the Nonintervention Committee.

In sum, the department's response to the Nonintervention Committee reveals a desire to avoid involvement in the Spanish civil war. The American position, as formulated by the State Department, supported the Nonintervention Committee with independent but parallel action.

A second major issue the State Department faced was whether to participate in international mediation efforts to end the Spanish civil war. Once again, the department turned down all such invitations, though it extended moral support to such endeavors at the end of 1936. Officials reacted to mediation proposals in the same way they responded to the Nonintervention Committee.

Mediation proposals during the Spanish conflict came from Latin American states and from European states. Of these two sources, the State Department was more concerned with those emanating from Latin America because of its concern with the impact of that war on Latin America. As Ambassador Bowers pointed out, "I have since coming here been profoundly impressed with the spiritual relationship, or perhaps I should call it the cultural relationship, between Spain and the South American republics that mean so much to us."[28] Moreover, the direct investments of the United States in Latin America amounted to nearly $3 billion. The department feared the influence on South American states of political developments in Spain.[29]

A government in Madrid containing socialists, communists, and anarchists offered a dangerous example to Latin

America. Therefore, many officials feared Bolshevism in Spain and supported Franco's cause. Five days after the outbreak of the civil war, for example, Hull wired Roosevelt; "One of the most serious factors in this situation lies in the fact that the [Spanish] Government has distributed large quantities of arms and ammunition into the hands of irresponsible members of left-wing political organizations."[30] In the same fashion, Ambassador Bullitt cautioned Roosevelt that events in Spain awakened the possibility that European civilization might be destroyed by Bolshevism.[31]

The department received invitations from Uruguay and Argentina to participate in mediation. On August 17, 1936, the Uruguayan minister approached Acting Secretary Phillips with a mediation offer. In his conversation with Phillips, the minister referred to a formal invitation from the Uruguayan minister of foreign affairs to the secretary of state, which the department had not yet received. In response to the minister's oral invitation, Phillips "reminded the Minister ... that the Department's position had been very clearly set forth in its circular instructions to diplomatic and consular officers in Spain on August 7th and that the country, as a whole, both Democratic and Republican press, had seemed to accept our position as the proper one." Once the department received the written invitation, Phillips wrote in reply: "After most careful consideration of all the circumstances involved we are constrained to believe that the prospect that such an offer as is suggested, would serve a useful purpose, is not such as to warrant a departure by this Government from its well established policy."[32] Again the department referred to the circular instructions of August 7, the basic document of American policy toward the Spanish civil war.

A second invitation to participate in a mediation scheme came from the Argentine ambassador, dean of the diplomatic corps in Spain. The ambassador proposed that the corps meet to discuss the possibility of offering mediation to the contending parties in Spain. When Bowers learned of the idea, he contacted the department and asked that he "be

instructed that since at this juncture the matter of intervention is premature I should not associate myself with the
meeting. I am sure we should not associate ourselves with
any mediation or intervention maneuver since this Civil
War is developing into a European quarrel." The same day,
Acting Secretary Phillips sent Bowers the following instructions: "While the American Government deplores the terri-
ble strife in Spain and devoutly wishes for peace at the
earliest possible moment, our policy, as already announced,
is to 'scrupulously refrain from any interference whatever in
the unfortunate Spanish situation.' (See telegraphic circular
of August 7 last.) In these circumstances, you should not
attend this proposed meeting."[33] The reaction of both Bowers and Phillips to the Argentine proposal demonstrates that
during the first year of the war they, like the rest of the
department, wanted to avoid involvement in what was regarded as a European quarrel. The exchange also shows once
again that the initial statement of the department's attitude
on August 7 was the basis of American policy toward Spain.

By the end of the year, the State Department modified
somewhat its attitude toward mediation offers. At that time
Britain and France approached the United States. On December 5, 1936, the French ambassador, in a conversation
with Acting Secretary Moore, delivered a mediation proposal identical to one presented by the British ambassador
on the previous day. Essentially, the message related that
the British and French governments would approach the
German, Italian, Portuguese, and Soviet governments to
stop war materiel from reaching Spain and suggest that
mediation be extended to the contesting parties. Moore told
the French ambassador there might be some hesitancy on
the part of the United States to have its representatives go
so far as to urge the states approached to accept the Anglo-
French proposal. Furthermore, since the president and the
secretary of state were away, a decision regarding the
American attitude would have to await their consideration.[34] Several days later, Hull conveyed his views on the
matter to the officials in Washington. As James Clemment
Dunn, chief of the Western European Division, related in

one memorandum, "It was evident ... that the Secretary entirely agreed with the Acting Secretary that no direct action should be taken in the capitals of the four countries to be approached and that it would perhaps be better not to take any action whatever in the matter until public announcement of the initiative had been made by the British and French Governments." Dunn, under instruction from Moore, told the British and French ambassadors that the entire issue had been presented to Roosevelt and that the acting secretary could give no opinion as to the president's decision.[35]

In the meantime, Moore contacted Roosevelt, and the president approved his reply to the Anglo-French proposal. After receiving presidential endorsement, the acting secretary instructed Dunn to inform the British and French of the government's position. Dunn complied. On December 9, he told the British and French ambassadors that the administration would not take any action until they publicly announced their mediation offer. Once announced, the acting secretary would be prepared, in response to inquiries from the press, to express the hope that some solution to the Spanish conflict would be found. Dunn went on to say that the president and the secretary of state were fully informed about the procedure and supported it and that the action once taken would become the official expression of the American government.[36] He released the department's statement on December 10: "It is the very earnest hope of our Government that the six nations mentioned may find a peaceful method of accomplishing the great purpose in view. This expression represents no deviation from our well-known policy of non-interference in the affairs of other countries."[37] Though extending moral support to the Anglo-French mediation scheme, the statement did not represent a change in departmental policy. Noninterference, a slogan used throughout the first year of the Spanish civil war, again defined the American position.

A third significant issue the State Department struggled with during 1936 was the problem of curtailing the shipment or transshipment of American arms and ammunition to

Spain. The problem assumed greater significance when Mexico, the Latin American state most sympathetic to the Republican government in Spain, became the base for the reshipment of American war materiel.

Mexican support for the Loyalist regime derived from the similar political experiences of the two regimes. The Mexican revolution of 1910, like developments in Spain in 1935, had been an uprising against the privileged position of lay and ecclesiastical classes.[38] As a result, when the Loyalist government appealed for aid, Mexico responded.[39] The department knew of Mexican aid to Spain as early as August 20. Josephus Daniels, the American ambassador to Mexico, wrote Hull that the Mexican government was sending munitions and that Eduardo Hay, the Mexican minister of foreign affairs, had assured him that the shipment contained no munitions purchased in the United States; all were manufactured in Mexico.[40]

The department did not object to the Mexican shipments of war materiel until products from the United States became involved. In September, the Mexican ambassador, acting under instructions from his government, asked if the United States would allow his country to purchase American-made arms for shipment to the Spanish government. Edward L. Reed, chief of the Division of Mexican Affairs, stated, "He was sure that the Ambassador must understand from the various statements that had been issued from the Department that the United States Government would certainly not be disposed to encourage the shipment of arms and munitions to either of the contending parties in Spain." Thereupon, Reed contacted Hull, who agreed that the Mexicans should be discouraged.[41]

A more serious problem with Mexico developed in December. The State Department learned of attempts to export American planes to Spain via Mexico. Moore then authorized the American chargé in Mexico, Pierre Boal, to inform Mexican authorities that if the planes were exported with a license naming Mexico as the country of destination for a temporary sojourn there pending transshipment, it consti-

tuted a violation of American law. Moore suggested points
Boal might add: "that his Government would appreciate any
action which the Mexican Government might feel at liberty
to take as an act of international courtesy to assist this
Government in the enforcement of its laws respecting international traffic in arms. You might remind the Mexican
authorities of the importance which they have always attached to the strict enforcement of our laws in respect to
arms leaving this country for Mexico."[42]

The State Department also endeavored to prevent American citizens from shipping arms and ammunition to Spain.
But because the neutrality act applied only to wars between
states, the department had no legal authority to prevent
such exports. Even the department's formal announcement
of policy on August 11 admitted that "our Neutrality Law
with respect to embargo of arms, ammunition and implements of war has no application in the present situation, since that applies only in the event of war *between or
among nations.*" For that reason, the department resorted
to a voluntary embargo, embodied in the statement:
"We believe that American citizens, both at home and
abroad, are patriotically observing this well-recognized
policy."[43]

Most department officials, as well as the president, supported a voluntary embargo policy. Hornbeck did not. In a
memorandum submitted on August 11, the chief of the Far
Eastern Division pointed out that a recognized government
had the right to purchase arms abroad and that the American government and American nationals had a right to sell
arms to any recognized government. Hornbeck asked:
"Would not the placing of a prohibition by the American
Government upon sale of arms by American nationals to the
Spanish Government or to both of the contending groups in
Spain, insofar as it interfered with the right of the Spanish
Government to purchase arms amount to an action of intervention by the American Government?"[44] Here Hornbeck
stated what several of his colleagues were to say in retro-
spect: that the government's policy of noninterference—

along with the voluntary embargo—was in reality intervention.

Hornbeck regarded the American policy in Spain as both dangerous and impractical. In a second memorandum on August 11, he argued that the administration had set a precedent that might embarrass the government when pursuing a contrary policy in other parts of the world, in particular the Far East. He wrote:

> The executive branch of the American Government should be prepared to feel that the same attitude should be taken in case of civil conflict in countries other than Spain. But, such is not the position that we have taken and that we do maintain with regard to civil conflict in certain other countries, conspicuously China. Prohibition by processes of persuasion rather than by authority under law is a very unsatisfactory and dangerous procedure from [the] point of view of political considerations and from [the] point of view of potential effectiveness.[45]

As an alternative, Hornbeck suggested the administration should obtain enabling legislation. In the absence of such authority, the government could not prevent the sale of arms to the parties in the Spanish civil war. As events developed, Hornbeck proved to be correct. The voluntary embargo was challenged, and the administration ultimately adopted his recommendation and asked Congress for covering legislation.

Most of the policy makers within the department did not share Hornbeck's view. Practically everyone else supported a voluntary embargo policy. Roosevelt endorsed Hull's Spanish policy, including the moral embargo. In his Chatauqua speech on August 14, 1936, he praised Hull as "that wise and experienced man who is our Secretary of State, whose statesmanship has met with such wide approval ... [who has] thought and worked long and hard on the problem of keeping the United States at peace."[46] Welles also supported

Hull's policy. In a speech before the Foreign Policy Association in New York on October 19, he declared: "Neutrality legislation has been devised by the Congress, intended to minimize the danger of the United States being drawn into wars in whose origins it has had no part."[47] Hull believed that a policy that would prevent arms from being shipped from the United States served national and international efforts to maintain peace and end the conflict.[48]

Yet Hornbeck's assessment proved correct. At the end of 1936, the government's voluntary embargo was successfully challenged when an exporter insisted upon his legal rights to ship arms to Spain. Consequently, the State Department and the chief executive had to inaugurate more stringent measures, which culminated in the Neutrality Act of 1937.[49] That act made it illegal to export arms and munitions to either side in a civil war.

The department followed the same approach in the Spanish civil war as it had followed in the Italo-Ethiopian war, to avoid American involvement at all costs. In so doing, the department went beyond traditional neutrality and isolationism. Ordinarily, during insurrections, the government in power can purchase supplies to suppress a rebellion. The nonintervention agreement in regard to Spain and the parallel American policy of noninterference denying the Loyalists access to war materiel departed from that practice. Of greater consequence was the noticeable departure in the department's attitude toward neutrality. Earlier, at the time of the arms embargo controversy, the department supported what might be called traditional isolationism. Officials accepted legislation avoiding American entanglements in Europe as long as the president retained the discretionary power to determine when involvement was necessary to the national interest. For that reason they opposed a neutrality policy that tied the president's hands. But by the time of both the Italo-Ethiopian war and the war in Spain, the department had shifted to the congressional position, to avoid any and all wars. By 1936, the department joined forces with the advocates of what may be called insulationism, supporting policies designed to prevent any of the extreme changes in the world's political climate from drawing the United States into foreign conflicts.

The consequences of the State Department's recommendations of 1936 were tragic because they were accepted and remained the American position for the balance of the civil war in Spain. A legitimate government was deprived of the material support it needed from the United States to suppress a fascist-oriented rebellion. Moreover, Franco's triumph encouraged other and more awesome fascist states to believe they need not fear American opposition to their designs. For all practical purposes, the department had become the defender of congressional neutrality legislation in response to world politics.

9. A Final Appraisal

During the early New Deal years, the Department of State participated in the design and conduct of foreign policy. At that time Roosevelt was not as involved in policy making as he was during World War II. He sought the advice of Secretary Hull and others, though he often ignored the department in his search for ideas, thus causing Hull difficult moments. But there was substantially less presidential control over policy than in later years. Hull's claim that he was not a functionary who carried messages to and from foreign governments is correct, once his difficulties with Moley and other rivals are discounted as part of his initiation process.

Hull's devotion to the reciprocal trade program, his grand design for world peace and prosperity, blunted his effectiveness as secretary of state. His almost monomaniacal devotion to that cause distracted him when other issues needed attention. Consequently, Hull deferred to subordinates on many matters, which enhanced their prestige and influence with Roosevelt and undercut Hull's authority. He erroneously assumed that career officers who were experienced specialists ipso facto possessed special wisdom; and he was unnecessarily deferential to their judgment.

The secretary might have taken instruction from Roosevelt. The president's eclectic approach to domestic problems carried over to some degree to foreign policy. Although Roosevelt never exhibited the same freewheeling experimentation in foreign policy matters that he did in domestic affairs, he encouraged advisers with entirely different opinions to believe that he was in complete agreement with them. That tactic was frustrating to them at times, especially to Hull, but Roosevelt's method had the advantage of keeping the department alert and in its place. Hull also failed to recognize Roosevelt's perception of effective administration. In a government where bureaucratic decision making is a fact, effective administration requires that a distinction be made between the advice of a skilled specialist and the wisdom of an experienced generalist. In short, Roosevelt was master of his own bureaucratic chaos; Hull was not.

If subordinate members of the State Department had possessed both the skill of diplomatic technicians and the judgment of wise diplomatists, Hull's practice of delegating authority would have been justified. Unfortunately, in most cases the career men in the department lacked imagination. Their foreign policy recommendations were carry-overs from the Hoover administration in particular and the remains of earlier misjudgments in general. From Hoover's secretary of state, Stimson, for example, they learned how to ignore Far Eastern realities and continued the nonrecognition approach to developments in Manchuria. That policy failed when Hoover was in office but was advocated nevertheless by Hornbeck and Grew during the Roosevelt administration. And the Far Eastern policy of Stimson was an extension of the Open Door policy, which had originated at the turn of the century.

In 1900 Secretary of State John Hay, in response to the division of China into spheres of economic and political influence by the major European powers, advocated a seemingly liberal alternative. He proposed that those countries with spheres of influence open trade while respecting the legitimacy of the spheres and, curiously, respecting Chinese sovereignty as well.

It was a confused policy. How could Chinese sovereignty be respected while spheres of foreign control of her territory existed? The inherent contradiction in the Open Door policy was ignored when the Washington Disarmament Conference met in 1922. The Nine Power Treaty, which grew out of that conference, legitimized the principle of the Open

Door. Obvious inconsistencies were removed; there were no more spheres of influence, but contradictions remained. By the 1930s, the Chinese government did not exercise effective control over the northern provinces, where warlords created a state of anarchy. A policy that respected what did not exist —Chinese sovereignty—and advocated what could not be— free trade with a country in turmoil—was absurd. The absurdity went unrecognized by the department. Instead, it blindly adhered to a treaty that had little to do with reality. Advisers with closed minds perpetuated the Open Door policy in the 1930s.

The department was also closed-minded in Latin American policy. Once again it continued a policy whose immediate antecedent was in the Hoover period but, like the Open Door, had earlier origins. The Hoover-Stimson approach to Latin American problems was to change the rhetoric of diplomacy, not the essence of foreign policy.

When Roosevelt was elected, he continued the approach of Hoover, which on the surface appeared to be a marked departure from the interventionism of the past. In his inaugural address, Roosevelt declared: "I would dedicate this nation to the policy of the good neighbor—the neighbor who resolutely respects himself and, because he does so, respects the rights of others—the neighbor who respects his obligations and respects the sanctity of his agreements in and with a world of neighbors." But Roosevelt's administration, like Hoover's, did not depart from the past. Hoover continued the Nicaraguan intervention, and Roosevelt supported intervention in Cuba. Admittedly, Roosevelt, in response to a growing Pan-American movement and later to an emerging Axis threat, shifted to more concrete expressions of neighborliness. But the tradition of maintaining a special position of dominance in the Western Hemisphere was continued, in keeping with the self-serving aspects of the Monroe Doctrine tradition.

A positive element of the Monroe Doctrine of 1823 restated a position enunciated by George Washington—to remain aloof from European entanglements, which were of no

concern to the United States. Neither Washington's Farewell Address nor Monroe's address to Congress (the "doctrine") excluded the possibility of involvement in European
affairs when warranted. But both statements advised an attitude of reserve, of great circumspection in regard to European politics.

That traditional reserve was well observed until Woodrow
Wilson departed from it in his Fourteen Points for peace to
end World War I. In particular, Wilson worked for the principle of collective security, the very antithesis of isolation, at
the Versailles peace conference after the war. Collective security became part of the peace treaty but was rejected by
the Senate. That rejection was not only a reaction to the
immediate circumstances of the debate over the ratification
of the Versailles Treaty. It marked the revival of an older
position, which disillusionment with the war had reinforced.

In the 1920s, under Republican leadership, that policy did
not change in any fundamental way. Alternatives to the
entanglement of participation in the League were sought.
The Kellogg-Briand agreement to outlaw war as an instrument of national policy and disarmament were the alternatives pursued. These devices, it was assumed, would make
unnecessary future involvement in European embroilments.

At the outset of the New Deal there was no genuine
attempt to deviate from the diplomacy of the preceding Republican era. There was no resurgence of Wilsonian international vigilantism in the form of collective security.
Disarmament remained a favored approach. When the department suggested that the United States might agree not
to interfere with collective pressure against an aggressor at
the time of the arms embargo discussions, it made clear that
such an agreement would be expressly contingent upon a
general disarmament agreement. Subsequently, when Congress passed neutrality legislation, the policy of isolation
became its own *reductio ad absurdum* of no political involvement under any circumstances.

At first the department demurred from the absolute congressional stand, but it supported the congressional view of

European policy at the time of the Italo-Ethiopian war and the Spanish civil war. Although neutrality legislation was clearly unneutral and isolationism was, by these laws, transformed into insulationism, there was no essential change in the attitude toward avoiding entanglement in Europe.

Devotion to these three policies—the Open Door, the aggressive aspects of the Monroe Doctrine tradition, and insulationism—was part of a more fundamental weakness in State Department thinking—the tendency to compartmentalize policy. In his discussion of the foreign policy of the 1930s, William W. Kaufmann writes:

> The idea that the United States might formulate a comprehensive program of action and then bring influence to bear in order to implement it was quite alien to the principal inhabitants of the State Department. Intimates of high officials have in fact expressed perfectly their philosophy during this period by saying that policy was the product of cables received from abroad rather than of a dynamic conception of American interests.

Kaufmann attributes this weakness to a lack of experience on the part of the professionals (they had had nothing to do for such a long time), and, more important, to inadequate political analysis stemming from the habit of seeing other nations "in their own image,"[1] that is, in the image of the United States. Kaufmann's interpretation has merit, but the inadequate political analysis he refers to probably revealed a pigeonhole perspective on nations and events rather than a solipsistic philosophy of government. Instead of a comprehensive view, international problems were seen in regional terms and policy was developed accordingly, for example, for the Far East, for Latin America, and for Europe. Rarely do we find a high-level department official cautioning that policy in one area might affect decisions in another area. From time to time Hornbeck attempted to show these interrelationships, but for the most part he limited his warnings to the ramifications of policy elsewhere on the Far East. The only comprehensive policy the department recommended was the reciprocal trade program, and that was equally narrow in its own way. Hull's mind was ruminative, not incisive; consequently, he did not see the complex interaction of currency, prices, trade, and politics. Overall, the thinking of the State Department lacked sophistication.

Equally unfortunate was the department's confusion of diplomacy with foreign policy, a serious lack of understanding reflected in the department's proposals of the means-end relationship. Extending or withholding recognition of another government, for example, is a diplomatic technique to achieve some larger purpose. At times this device was used to the point of foolishness or abuse. Nonrecognition in the Far East served no useful purpose. Denying that the Japanese puppet state Manchukuo existed did not alter events there in any way. American economic interests in Manchukuo did not improve, nor did relations with Japan change as a result. Since sanctions of any kind were out of the question, adherence to the nonrecognition formula was foolish. Under the circumstances, the department might have recommended recognition along with a proposal for a quid pro quo that would protect American interests. That alternative was never given very serious consideration by the department.

Withholding recognition of the Grau San Martin regime in Cuba was more potent in effect than the Far Eastern policy but certainly was not in keeping with a good neighbor policy. In Africa the use of recognition was equally unproductive. It was not the withholding of recognition per se that persuaded the Liberians to accept United States control over their country's economy and government. Without American economic support the bankrupt Liberians could not function. On the east coast of Africa, in Ethiopia, where there might have been some merit to refusing to recognize the Italian conquest, the department bowed to the inevitable and recommended extending recognition to the new regime immediately. Accepting imperialism in Africa while rejecting it in the Far East did little to enhance respect for the United States in the Axis camp.

Confusion of method and goal was equally plain in the department's attitude toward the recognition of the Soviet Union. Withholding recognition until satisfaction was given on the comparatively minor points of debts and personal freedom for Americans in Russia was the accepted view of the department. Fortunately, Roosevelt ignored that opinion. He saw the broader political implications involved in restoring normal relations with a power that could not go unnoticed in the emerging scheme of international relationships.

The reliance on nonrecognition reveals another weakness in the State Department's approach to international issues. Diplomacy is, after all, only one of the devices to achieve the national interest. It exists side by side with, and is dependent upon, the use of force. In a retrospective interview, Hornbeck leveled this criticism against Grew and against the idea that diplomacy alone is sufficient:

> Mr. Grew was a diplomat's diplomat. Mr. Grew was a firm believer in the efficacy of diplomacy. He believed that negotiation could resolve any problem in international relations. Most of specialists in the Division of Far Eastern Affairs did not share Mr. Grew's faith in diplomacy. Some matters, for example, such as an attempted hold-up or various personal rivalries cannot be solved by diplomacy. There can be no compromise; either you lose your money or you lose your girl or you resort to force. The same is true in foreign affairs. Some issues cannot be solved by talk, only by force or the threat of force and such was the case in the light of Japanese purposes in American relations with Japan.[2]

Hornbeck's criticism is very much to the point and reflects his ability to present, on occasion, a minority view in the department. Nevertheless, his observation is ironic in light of his own behavior, in regard to Far Eastern policy at least.

Hornbeck endorsed the continuation of the nonrecognition formula and discouraged using the mildest sanctions. Yet to resist from a position of weakness runs counter to elementary diplomatic logic. And so the cables and memorandums emanating from the Far Eastern Division of the department formed the collage of a paper tiger.

Far Eastern policy was not unique in this regard. Disarmament was advocated by officials concerned with developments in Europe. With the exception of the Cuban situation, even a show of force anywhere was out of the question as far as the State Department was concerned.

From time to time in examinations on various issues, including the need to strengthen the navy, alternatives to existing policy were heard from a few department policy makers. For the most part, there was nothing new in their thinking. Here Roosevelt cannot be blamed for discouraging new ideas. To a large extent, Hull's claim that Roosevelt was distracted by domestic problems, thereby allowing Hull and the department a wide range of authority, is substantially correct. The president's eventual endorsement of the reciprocal trade program reveals at least some tolerance of innovation in foreign affairs that might have been expanded to embrace other equally imaginative policies. Of course, we will never know if alternatives would have worked. Nevertheless, in contrast to the furious if sometimes frivolous experimentation in domestic affairs, the conduct of foreign policy at the hands of the department was singularly lethargic. In reality, therefore, the term "New Deal diplomacy" is a misnomer. It was an old deal that varied little in either conception or execution from what had gone before.

Epilogue

On October 5, 1937, President Roosevelt proposed in a speech in Chicago that the peace-loving nations of the world quarantine the aggressor nations. Although there is controversy among historians as to what the statement meant, some evidence suggests that Roosevelt had in mind a long-range naval blockade of Japan.[1] Whatever his immediate intentions, it is clear that after 1937 Roosevelt became more active in foreign policy making than he had been earlier. From that point on, the State Department's role in designing policy diminished.

The "Quarantine" speech is a line of demarcation in New Deal diplomacy. Before 1937 world politics were relatively fluid. But gradually from 1933 to 1937 the situation solidified so that by the time Roosevelt proposed to quarantine aggressor states, the foreign policy of the United States started to take on the character of wartime diplomacy. With the formation of the alliance between Italy, Germany, and Japan in 1936; the withdrawal of Italy from the League of Nations in 1937; the German seizure of Austria and the capitulation to Nazi interests in Czechoslovakia in 1938; and the German invasion of Poland in 1939, which led to the declaration of war by Britain and France, it was essential to adjust American foreign policy to the breakdown of international order. Roosevelt and Congress finally reversed noninterventionist American policy with the Neutrality Act of 1939, which repealed the mandatory arms embargo and thereby enabled the export of arms and munitions to nations resisting aggression.

Thus the history of American foreign policy before 1937

may be regarded as a time of missed opportunity, and the State Department was as responsible as the president for the failure. I agree with the "realist" critics of American foreign policy in their criticism of the tendency to allow abstract general principles, especially moral ones, to govern decisions in the realm of foreign affairs.[2] But I do not accept their contention that only the career diplomat should be entrusted with charting the course the nation should take.[3] During the early New Deal period the career men in the department were no more effective than elected or appointed officials. They also suffered from weaknesses which the "realists" deplore: they proclaimed general principles, they offered simplistic solutions, and they participated in some of the flashier aspects of diplomacy which have little real effect such as international gatherings or conferences. In sum, there was a lack of understanding, imagination, and boldness at a time when such qualities might have altered the course of events leading to World War II.

Notes

PREFACE

1. Like Martin Weil, I believe the State Department was influential before 1937; see Weil, *A Pretty Good Club,* pp. 85-86.
2. Robert Dallek, *Franklin D. Roosevelt and American Foreign Policy, 1932-1945;* Robert A. Divine, *The Illusion of Neutrality;* Dorothy Borg, *The United States and the Far Eastern Crisis of 1933-1938;* and Armin Rappaport, *Henry L. Stimson and Japan, 1931-1933.*
3. Herbert Feis, *1933.*

CHAPTER 1

1. Herbert Feis, *1933,* pp. 5-6.
2. Ibid., pp. 5-7.
3. Lloyd C. Gardner, *Economic Aspects of New Deal Diplomacy,* pp. 7-10.
4. Feis, *1933,* pp. 9, 13.
5. See Gardner, *Economic Aspects of New Deal Diplomacy,* p. 14; Raymond Moley, *After Seven Years,* p. 48; and Feis, *1933,* p. 104.
6. *Congressional Record,* 62d Cong., 1st sess., June 9, 1911, vol. 47, pt. 2, pp. 1811-12.
7. Ibid., 65th Cong., 3d sess., Feb. 21, 1919, vol. 57, pt. 4, p. 3955.
8. Ibid., 68th Cong., 1st sess., March 11, 1924, vol. 55, pt. 4, p. 3947.
9. Cordell Hull, *The Memoirs of Cordell Hull,* 1:191.
10. Feis, *1933,* pp. 21-22.
11. Ibid., p. 22.
12. Ibid., p. 23.
13. Ibid., pp. 23-24.
14. Ibid., p. 25.
15. Ibid., p. 26.
16. Ibid., p. 28.
17. For a discussion on the attempt at liaison between the two administrations, see Feis, *1933,* chaps. 3-9.
18. Ibid., pp. 132, 142.

19. Ibid., pp. 145, 148, 150-51, 169.

20. *New York Times,* May 21, 1933, p. 29. From the beginning it was clear to some career men in the department that Moley was "in" but not "of" the department. See Nancy Harvison Hooker, ed., *The Moffat Papers,* pp. 89-90. Also see Jay Pierrepont Moffat Diary, May 16, 1933, in which he describes Moley as independent, not at all conciliatory, and one who does not fit in an organization.

21. Feis observed, "What a motley group, I thought as I read the roster. But as the saying goes, I had not seen anything yet. No reflection of mine could be more pertinent than the one made by Moley after the fiasco: 'It's doubtful whether a collection of the political geniuses of all the ages could have represented us satisfactorily under these circumstances. But the odds were a million to one that the delegation Roosevelt chose could not negotiate satisfactorily on the basis of these confused, confusing, shifting purposes' " (Feis, *1933,* p. 174). But Feis was particularly upset with Pittman. "He was mean. Although chairman of the Committee on Foreign Relations, he cared little or nothing about any other foreign country. His interest in monetary policies was centered on improving the prices and prospects of silver mined in Nevada and neighboring states" (ibid., p. 173).

22. Ibid., pp. 175-76, 194.

23. Ibid., p. 181.

24. Ibid., pp. 188-89.

25. Ibid., p. 199.

26. Ibid., pp. 200-07.

27. Ibid., pp. 212-13.

28. Feis believes that Hull was reacting to Moley's meetings with the prime minister and other major officials without Hull's permission (ibid., p. 226).

29. Ibid., pp. 235, 237-38.

30. Ibid., pp. 249-50. Bingham was also the source of rumors about Moley's conduct and expense account.

31. After the "bombshell message," the president cabled the American delegation: "First, I think you can make definite offers to any nations to discuss with us reciprocal tariff agreements in Washington at their convenience" (President Roosevelt to the American Delegation, July 4, 1933, 550.S1 Economic Commission). Hereafter all citations followed by file numbers refer to unpublished records of the Department of State, National Archives.

In mid-July, Roosevelt expressed interest in the trade program and anticipated tariff reductions (see Moffat diary, July 12, 1933). At the time of the bombshell message, the State Department formulated a series of proposals designed to save the conference: a prolonged tariff truce, a multilateral agreement to reduce tariff duties, and a multilateral agreement to abolish import quotas (Memorandum from the Office of the Economic Adviser to Phillips, July 13, 1933, 550.S1 Economic Commission). See also Hull to Roosevelt, July 2, 1933, 220.S1 Economic Commission; Hull to Roosevelt, July 30, 1933, 550.S1 Economic Commission.

32. Feis's sympathy to Hull is evident throughout his book, even though he did not think Hull particularly clever (*1933*, chaps. 17-20). Feis believed the "depth and durability of Hull's hatred [toward Moley] was extreme" (ibid., p. 248).

Francis B. Sayre, an assistant secretary of state, recalls, "In June, 1933, President Roosevelt sent Mr. Hull to the London Economic Conference as America's top representative; shortly after, he sent Mr. Moley as his personal representative, regardless of the fact that the two held views directly in conflict. Only shipwreck could result. For this and other reasons the London Conference ended in failure. . . . All this meant heartache and sometimes tense conflict for Secretary Hull. A man of smaller stature, fearing he had lost the confidence of the President, would have resigned. But Mr. Hull, steadfast and unflinching, did not" (*Glad Adventure*, p. 161).

33. Hull, *Memoirs*, 1:317-18.

34. The *Department of State Press Releases*, Oct. 28, 1933, pp. 239-43.

35. Instructions to the Delegates to the Seventh International Conference of American States, Montevideo, Nov. 10, 1933, *Foreign Relations of the United States, Diplomatic Papers, 1933*, 4:85.

36. William Phillips Diary, Nov. 28, 1933; also ibid., Dec. 13, 1933; Hull, *Memoirs*, 1:321-22.

37. *New York Times*, Dec. 13, 16, 1933.

38. Ibid., Dec. 16, 1933, p. 42. See also Josephus Daniels to Roosevelt, July 15, 1933, in Edgar B. Nixon, ed., *Franklin D. Roosevelt and Foreign Affairs*, 1:313.

39. Phillips diary, April 3, 1934.

40. Ibid. See also Moffat to John Campbell White, Feb. 6, 1934, Moffat Papers; R. Walton Moore to Cordell Hull, Dec. 29, 1933, Cordell Hull Papers; Josephus Daniels to Cordell Hull, July 24, 1934, ibid.

41. Bryce Wood defines the Good Neighbor policy as reciprocity or the Golden Rule in foreign policy. He is correct in maintaining that "the idea of reciprocity expressed the hope that if the United States did certain things desired by Latin American states, these states would respond by doing other things desired by Washington. . . . For nonintervention and noninterference, would not Latin American governments respond by 'equitable' treatment for the property of United States citizens and corporations?" (*The Making of the Good Neighbor Policy*, pp. 7-8). But Wood goes too far when he tries to explain the contradictions in the Good Neighbor policy: "The idea of the anticipation of reciprocity, which has been suggested as the basic conception of the United States government from 1933 onward in its relations with Latin America, was supplemented in 1939 and afterward by an idea that may be called the evocation of reciprocity" (ibid., p. 390). The goal of Latin American policy remained economic expansion. As Sumner Welles recalls, "Throughout the period between the inauguration of the Good

Neighbor Policy and the outbreak of war in 1939, a large part of the work
of creating the new inter-American relationship had been taken up with the
economic and financial considerations" (*The Time for Decision,* p. 209). I
agree with Paul A. Varg, who sees the reciprocal trade program as contrary
to the "Good Neighbor" euphemism. See Varg, "The Economic Side of the
Good Neighbor Policy," and Allen F. Repko, "The Failure of Reciprocal
Trade."

42. Memorandum, Moore to Hull, Nov. 6, 1933, and attached letter of
Daniels to Hull, Oct. 17, 1933, R. Walton Moore Papers. Assistant Secretary
of State Moore expressed disagreement with Daniels's suggestion.

43. When this committee was set up, some members of the State Department believed too many new government agencies were involved with foreign trade, the traditional concern of the department (Phillips diary, Nov.
2, 1933).

44. Phillips wrote in his diary, "Our policy here, in the circumstances,
is to sit quietly in the firm belief that things will work out all right and that
probably Peek will not be in the game very long" (Dec. 12, 1933).

45. Peek used similar tactics when he was in the Department of Agriculture (ibid., Jan. 4, 1934).

46. Ibid., State Department memorandum, Jan. 8, 1934, Hull Papers.
Some of the economic advisers in the department felt that there was nothing to worry about (Moffat diary, Feb. 27, 1934; Phillips diary, Feb. 27, 1934).

47. Hull, *Memoirs,* 1:377. In the department there was widespread satisfaction with the legislation. Sumner Welles recalls, for example, "The
greatest positive achievement of the first Roosevelt Administration in the
realm of international cooperation lay in the trade agreements policy for
which [the] Secretary of State is wholly responsible" (Welles, *Time for
Decision,* p. 55).

48. Memorandum, Roosevelt to Cordell Hull, Nov. 19, 1934, Hull Papers, Box 37.

49. Moffat diary, Nov. 20, 1934; *New York Times,* Nov. 21, 1934, p. 4,
Nov. 23, 1934, p. 5; Phillips diary, Nov. 22, 1934.

50. Phillips diary, Feb. 14, 19, 1935.

51. William E. Leuchtenburg, *Franklin D. Roosevelt and the New Deal,*
p. 205. Former Secretary of State Henry Stimson thought the tariff bill was
an opportunity to support the "conservative" advisers to the president and
to oppose the "radical" advisers (May 18, 1934, Stimson Diary, Vols. 27-28).

52. Richard N. Kottman, *Reciprocity and the North Atlantic Triangle,
1932–1938,* p. 274.

CHAPTER 2

1. Robert Paul Browder, *The Origins of Soviet-American Diplomacy,* p.
38; Joan H. Wilson, "American Business and the Recognition of the Soviet

Union," p. 36N; William E. Leuchtenburg, *Franklin D. Roosevelt and the New Deal,* p. 206.

2. Beatrice Farnsworth, *William C. Bullitt and the Soviet Union,* p. 13.

3. Ibid., p. 15.

4. Ibid., pp. 19, 55-57.

5. Ibid., p. 69.

6. *Browder, Origins of Soviet-American Diplomacy, p. 25.*

7. Ibid., p. 48.

8. Ibid., p. 69. See also Stimson to Senator William E. Borah, Sept. 8, 1932, Stimson Papers.

9. *FRUS, The Soviet Union, 1933–1939,* 2:781, 782.

10. Herbert Feis, *1933,* pp. 310-11.

11. See William Phillips, *Ventures in Diplomacy,* p. 156.

12. Farnsworth, *Bullitt,* p. 80.

13. Ibid., pp. 88-89.

14. Feis, *1933,* pp. 309-10; Farnsworth, *Bullitt,* p. 92; Browder, *Origins of Soviet-American Diplomacy,* John Morton Blum, *From the Morgenthau Diaries,* pp. 21, 56-57.

15. Kelley's memorandum is found in *FRUS, The Soviet Union,* pp. 6-13.

16. Ibid. Several days after Hull's memorandum was sent to the president, Kelley made an identical recommendation in a memorandum to Undersecretary Phillips (*FRUS, 1933,* 2:790-91). For a discussion of Kelley's opposition to the recognition of the Soviet Union see Hugh De Santis, *The Diplomacy of Silence,* p. 28. Apparently there was some concern in the State Department that Roosevelt might extend credits to ease the way for recognition (Feis, *1933,* pp. 311, 313).

17. Feis, *1933,* p. 313. For Russia's pressure for credits during the summer see Blum, *Morgenthau Diaries,* pp. 56-57.

18. See Phillips, *Ventures in Diplomacy,* p. 156.

19. See Feis, *1933,* p. 308. Bullitt ascribed the bias of the State Department to Secretary of State Hull's concern about the religious freedom issue (Blum, *Morgenthau Diaries,* p. 56). For an interesting observation on Kelley's influence see Daniel Yergin, *Shattered Peace,* p. 21.

20. *FRUS, 1933,* 2:792.

21. Ibid., p. 793.

22. Hull agreed; see Cordell Hull, *The Memoirs of Cordell Hull,* 1:297.

23. Feis, *1933,* p. 314.

24. Blum, *Morgenthau Diaries,* pp. 56-57.

25. Feis, *1933,* p. 315; Blum, *Morgenthau Diaries,* pp. 56-57. I believe Farnsworth's interpretation of the difference between the department, Bullitt, and the president is exaggerated. Beatrice Farnsworth, *William C. Bullitt and the Soviet Union,* ch. 5.

26. *FRUS, The Soviet Union,* p. 24.

27. Hull, *Memoirs,* 1:300.

28. For discussion of the Third International see Feis, *1933,* pp. 318-20, and Browder, *Origins of Soviet-American Diplomacy,* p. 131.

29. Farnsworth, *Bullitt,* p. 99.

30. Ibid., pp. 21, 105.

31. Ibid., p. 106.

32. Hull, *Memoirs,* 1:207.

33. Phillips, *Ventures in Diplomacy,* p. 158.

34. See Farnsworth, *Bullitt,* p. 109.

35. Orville H. Bullitt, ed., *For the President,* p. 67.

36. Ibid., quotation on p. 73; see p. 68.

37. Farnsworth, *Bullitt,* p. 111.

38. Bullitt to Hull, March 28, 1934, *FRUS, The Soviet Union,* p. 74.

39. Bullitt to Hull, March 15, 1934, ibid., pp. 66-67.

40. Farnsworth, *Bullitt,* p. 123.

41. Ibid., pp. 124-25.

42. Ibid., pp. 128, 130-31.

43. Ibid., p. 143.

44. *FRUS, The Soviet Union,* p. 29.

45. Bullitt, ed., *For the President,* pp. 130-31, letter to Roosevelt, July 15, 1935.

46. Ibid.

47. Ibid., p. 134, letter to Moore, July 15, 1935.

48. Farnsworth, *Bullitt,* p. 153.

49. See Kennan's introduction to Bullitt, ed., *For the President,* pp. vi, 64, 157.

50. Stanley K. Hornbeck to Cordell Hull, March 24, 1933, and memorandum by Hornbeck, March 24, 1933, Hornbeck Papers. See also Joan Hoff Wilson, *Ideology and Economics.* I agree with her conclusion. She maintains: "The policy of non-recognition also provides one of the best examples of twentieth century U.S. diplomacy at its worst because it fostered a lack of reconciliation and coordination between economic and political foreign policy. This inconsistency was the direct product of an ideologically based diplomacy that became bureaucratized and obsolete but nonetheless self-perpetuating" (p. 103).

CHAPTER 3

1. Robert F. Smith, *The United States and Cuba,* pp. 17-18, 41, 139. See also the excellent article by F. David Cronon, "Interpreting the New Good Neighbor Policy." I disagree with Jules R. Benjamin, who sees relations with Cuba in this period as a break with the past ("The New Deal, Cuba, and the Rise of a Global Economic Policy," p. 77).

2. Smith, *United States and Cuba,* pp. 137-38.

3. Ibid., pp. 118, 135.

4. Ibid., p. 141.

5. Although Welles's methods differed from those recommended by his superior, Secretary Hull, the two agreed about objectives. Before becoming secretary of state Hull had demonstrated that he favored American economic penetration in Cuba. In 1929 and 1930, as a senator, Hull had worked with the Cuban sugar lobby (ibid., p. 143).

6. Ambassador Welles to Hull, May 13, 1933, 837.00/3512.

7. Department of State, *Press Releases,* June 10, 1933, p. 434.

8. Despite Welles's obvious interventionist tactics, the State Department denied any interference in Cuban affairs. See Department of State, *Press Releases,* Sept. 9, 1933, pp. 141-47.

9. Welles to Hull, Aug. 8, 1933, 837.00/3616.

10. *New York Times,* Aug. 9, 1933, p. 1.

11. Welles to Hull, Aug. 30, 1933, 837.00/3739, for the ambassador's concern about the "red menace" and his request for military assistance; see transcribed long-distance telephone conversation between Hull and Welles, Sept. 5, 1933, 837.00/3800; Welles to Hull, Sept. 8, 1933, 837.00/3793; Welles to Hull, Sept. 8, 1933, 837.00/3785.

12. Welles to Hull, Sept. 8, 1933, 837.00/3798.

13. Daniels to Hull, Sept. 8, 1933, 837.00/4033.

14. Daniels to Hull, Sept. 14, 1933, Cordell Hull Papers, File Box 34. In another letter, Daniels argued, "The chief cause of the trouble in Cuba is the hunger of the people, due to sugar prices. Can our country escape part responsibility, seeing American interests own such a large per cent of plantations, mines, public service corporations and the like?" (Daniels to Hull, Sept. 18, 1933, ibid.).

15. William Phillips Diary, Nov. 6, 1933. For Phillips's desire to get Welles out of Cuba, see ibid., Dec. 12, 1933.

16. See Welles to Hull, Sept. 17, 1933, 837.00/3908.

17. Welles to Hull, telegram, Sept. 11, 1933, *FRUS, 1933,* 5:422-24. For other statements by the ambassador with regard to communist activities and threats to American property, see transcribed long-distance telephone conversation between Hull and Welles, Sept. 11, 1933, 837.00/3839, National Archives and Welles to Hull, Sept. 15, 1933, 837.00/3893, ibid.

18. Welles to Hull, Sept. 17, 1933, 837.00/3914; Welles to Hull, Sept. 18, 1933, 837.00/3934, ibid.

19. Welles to Hull, Oct. 16, 1933, 837.00/4206, ibid.

20. Phillips Diary, Nov. 25, 1933.

21. See Phillips, telegram to Hull, Nov. 28, 1933, *FRUS, 1933,* 5:527-28.

22. Phillips diary, Nov. 22, 1933; Department of State, *Press Releases,* Nov. 25, 1933, pp. 294-95.

23. Special Representative Caffery to Acting Secretary Phillips, Jan. 14, 1934, *FRUS, 1934,* 5:98, Hull also favored immediate recognition. See Phillips diary, Jan. 21, 1934.

24. In spite of his disapproval of Welles's diplomacy in Cuba, Phillips believed the trade agreement with Cuba (an outgrowth of Welles's intervention) was a good start in the anticipated series of agreements under the trade legislation.

25. Irwin F. Gellman, *Roosevelt and Batista,* concludes: "In the process of the evolution of the Good Neighbor Policy in Cuba, opposition forces rightly charged the United States with maintaining the status quo, and these attacks became part of a growing tradition of anti-American feeling" (p. 236).

26. Raymond W. Bixler, *The Foreign Policy of the United States in Liberia,* p. 13.

27. Ibid., pp. 15, 20-23, 29-34.

28. Indicative of the State Department's reaction to the plan was a memorandum written by Jay Pierrepont Moffat, chief of the Western European Division: "We have for some years taken the position that the American Government was not prepared to assume sole responsibility in securing reform in Liberia.... We have accordingly been members of the international committee on Liberia for some three or four years. That committee drew up a plan of assistance which we endorsed to the Firestones as offering the basis for further negotiations between Liberia and themselves. The plan set up a series of effective safeguards under the control of the Chief Adviser for whom we have obtained adequate authority" (Moffat, memorandum to Hull, May 11, 1933, Jay Pierrepont Moffat Papers).

29. For the text of the League Plan of Assistance, see League of Nations, "General Principles of the Plan of Assistance Drawn up by the Committee and Accepted by the Liberian Representatives," *Official Journal* 13 (Dec. 1932): 2053–54.

30. The Firestones, like President Hoover, favored gunboat diplomacy in Liberia (see Jay Pierrepont Moffat Diary, Jan. 23, 24, 1933). Although the department disavowed force, policy makers were determined to protect the Firestone Company by working with the League (ibid., Jan. 21, 27, 1933).

31. Stimson to Hoover, Feb. 24, 1933, 882.01 Winship/18. Cordell Hull endorsed Stimson's policy (Moffat diary, Feb. 27, 1933).

32. Excerpts of Winship's dispatch are in *FRUS, 1933,* 2:905, 882.01 Winship Mission/46. For the complete statement, see Winship to Hull, April 8, 1933, 882.01 Winship Mission/46. There was sentiment in the department in favor of Winship's suggestions. See Moffat, memorandum to Hull, May 11, 1933, Moffat Papers.

33. Moffat diary, May 12, June 28, July 15, 16, 1933.

34. Department of State, *Press Releases,* Aug. 5, 1933, pp. 71-72. For examples of attacks upon the department's policy, see W. E. Burghardt DuBois, "Liberia, the League and the United States"; Raymond Leslie Buell, "The New Deal and Liberia"; and Mauritz A. Hallgren, "Liberia in Shackles."

35. Moffat diary, Aug. 14, Sept. 8, 1933; Phillips to Roosevelt, Aug. 16, 1933, *FRUS, 1933*, 2:924-26, 882.01 Foreign Control/ 620a. Some members of the department did not take the criticism seriously. See Phillips, memorandum to Roosevelt, Aug. 15, 1933, Moffat Papers.

36. Moffat diary, Sept. 9, 10, 21, 1933.

37. Hull to Roosevelt, Sept. 21, 1933, *FRUS, 1933*, 2:933-34, 882.01 Foreign Control/656a.

38. Moffat diary, Sept. 23, 24, 1933. Secretary Hull supported the decision of his subordinates on this matter.

39. See League of Nations, "Statement by the American Representative," *Official Journal* 14 (Oct. 9, 1933): 1736; italics added.

40. Moffat diary, Oct. 30, Nov. 3, 1933. On November 13, Moffat wrote in his diary that the department intended to publicize Liberia's refusal "as a disinclination to accept reforms, the necessity of which had been recognized for years, and as an indifference to the welfare of the million and a half natives in that country."

41. For indications of the department's concern over the Rubber Restriction Agreement, see "The State Department's Activity for the Purpose of Safeguarding the United States Against the Rubber Shortage in the Event of an Emergency," May 22, 1942, Cordell Hull Papers, File Box 82; Phillips diary, Jan. 8, 1934; memorandum from the Office of the Economic Adviser to the secretary of state, Feb. 19, 1934, 856D.6176/142; memorandum from the Office of the Economic Adviser, Feb. 23, 1934, 856D.1176/181; memorandum from the undersecretary of state to the secretary of state, Feb. 27, 1934, 856D.6176/152.

42. For the text of the reservations, see League of Nations, *Official Journal,* 15 (June 1934): 561-62.

43. For indications of the department's confusion, see Moffat diary, May 2, 1934.

44. The suggestion to send McBride was made by Phillips and endorsed by Hull. See Phillips diary, June 9, 28, 1934.

45. Moffat diary, Aug. 27, 1934.

46. One part of the Liberian plan called for a temporary moratorium on loan payments. For the department's adverse reaction to this provision, see McBride to the secretary of state, Aug. 29, 1934, 882.01 Foreign Control/891; Moffat diary, Aug. 31, 1934.

47. See "Report by Harry A. McBride, Special Assistant to the Secretary of State, upon Conditions in Liberia," Oct. 3, 1934, *FRUS, 1934*, 2:806-15, 882.01 Foreign Control/915.

48. Members of the department believed that the Liberian government could be "influenced" by the American advisers under the provisions of the Liberian Plan. See Phillips diary, Oct. 22, 1934.

49. Smith, *United States and Cuba,* preface.

50. Daniels believed that some career men in the State Department were not in sympathy with the Good Neighbor policy, having internalized

the old order of "Speak softly and carry a big stick" (Daniels to Assistant
Secretary R. Walton Moore, March 27, 1936, Moore Papers).

CHAPTER 4

1. Cordell Hull, *The Memoirs of Cordell Hull,* 1:194.

2. Julius Pratt, *Cordell Hull,* 1:19, 25; Hull, *Memoirs,* 1:180-81, 185, 202.

3. Stanley K. Hornbeck, interview with author, Jan. 3, 1966. A text of
the interview, edited by Hornbeck, is in Howard Jablon, "Cordell Hull, the
State Department and the Foreign Policy of the First Roosevelt Administration, 1933–1936" (Ph.D. dissertation, Rutgers University, 1967), pp. 244-47.

4. Armin Rappaport, *Henry L. Stimson and Japan, 1931–1933,* pp. 38,
95. I agree with James C. Thomson, Jr., regarding Hornbeck's belief in the
Open Door; see Thomson, "The Role of the Department of State."

5. Stanley K. Hornbeck, "Manchuria Situation, Constant Factors for
Consideration in Connection with Problem of American-Japanese Relations," March 14, 1933, Hornbeck Papers, Hoover Institution; In 1933, Jay
Pierrepont Moffat, chief of the West European Division, stressed the role of
a strong American navy in maintaining peace in the Far East; see Moffat
to Joseph C. Grew, July 14, 1933, Moffat Papers. Also see Hornbeck, "Why
Not Abandon the Open Door Policy," April 13, 1935, and Hornbeck, "Foreign Policy of the United States, in Analysis with Suggestions for Proce-
dures," April 17, 1935, Franklin D. Roosevelt Library.

6. *FRUS, 1933,* 3:7-8.

7. Observations upon Stimson's policy have been drawn from throughout Rappaport's *Stimson and Japan.*

8. Henry L. Stimson, *The Far Eastern Crisis,* pp. 166-68.

9. Memorandum of conversation between Stimson and Roosevelt,
March 28, 1933, Stimson Papers; Herbert Feis, *1933,* pp. 57-59.

10. Henry L. Stimson and McGeorge Bundy, *On Active Service in Peace
and War,* pp. 294-95.

11. Hull, *Memoirs,* 1:270. See also Memorandum of conversation with
Secretary Hull, Jan. 1935, Stimson Papers.

12. Hull, *Memoirs,* 1:271-74.

13. Dorothy Borg, *The United States and the Far Eastern Crisis of 1933–
1938,* p. 25.

14. *FRUS, 1933,* 1:96-97.

15. Hull, *Memoirs,* 1:273.

16. Jay Pierrepont Moffat Diary, April 28, 1933; Davis, telegram to Hull,
April 27, 1933, *FRUS, 1933,* 1:116.

17. Memorandum by the Division of Far Eastern Affairs, March 7, 1933,
"Manchuria Situation, Proposed Embargo on Export of Arms, Bearing of

this Proposal, if Adopted and Acted upon on Relations of the United States with Countries of the Far East," 893.113/1467.

18. Grew, telegram to Hull, May 8, 1933, *FRUS, 1933*, 3:732-34.

19. Consul General (at Mukden) Myrl S. Myers to Phillips, July 10, 1933, ibid., pp. 736-37.

20. Grew, telegram to Hull, May 8, 1933.

21. Memorandum, Division of Far Eastern Affairs (and attached notes), Oct. 5, 1933, 692.113 Manchuria Petroleum/12.

22. Hull, *Memoirs*, 1:275-76.

23. Stanley K. Hornbeck, *Principles of American Policy in Relation to the Far East.*

24. Joseph C. Grew, *Turbulent Era*, pp. 953-54.

25. Memorandum by the chief of the Division of Far Eastern Affairs, Feb. 15, 1934, *FRUS, 1934*, 3:36-38.

26. Hornbeck, interview, Jan. 6, 1966.

27. In this connection, see the following: Memorandum, Division of Far Eastern Affairs, March 7, 1934, 693.113 (Manchuria) Petroleum/34; Joseph C. Grew Diary, April 25, 1934; Hull, telegram to Grew, April 28, 1934, 793.94/6625A.

28. Grew, telegram to Hull, Aug. 20, 1934, 893.6363 Manchuria/34; Grew diary, Aug. 1–19, 1934; Grew, *Turbulent Era*, p. 969.

29. Memorandum of a conversation between the secretary of the interior, Harold Ickes, and Hornbeck, Aug. 23, 1934, 894.6363/87; memorandum of a conversation between Phillips, Hornbeck, and Eugene H. Dooman, Aug. 23, 1934, 894.6363/86; Phillips diary, Aug. 24, 30, 1934; Phillips, telegram to Grew, Aug. 31, 1934, *FRUS, 1934*, 3:728-29.

30. Phillips diary, Sept. 21, 1934; Hull, telegram to Grew, Sept. 21, 1934, *FRUS, 1934*, 3:733. There was also a feeling in the department that the American oil companies would not cooperate in implementing an informal embargo (Phillips diary, Oct. 25, 1934; Phillips, telegram to Grew, Oct. 31, 1934, *FRUS, 1934*, 3:752).

31. *FRUS, Japan, 1931–1941*, 1:224.

32. Hornbeck, "Draft Reminiscences," Hornbeck Papers, Hoover Institution; Hull, *Memoirs*, 1:279; Phillips diary, April 19, 1934.

33. Memorandum by the chief of the Division of Far Eastern Affairs, April 24, 1934, 793.94/6728.

34. Hornbeck, "Draft Reminiscences."

35. Memorandum of the Division of Far Eastern Affairs, April 28, 1934, 793.94/6625 1/2. Phillips wanted the statement to contain references to international law and treaties (Phillips to Ambassador Bingham, April 23, 1934, *FRUS, Japan*, 1:126).

36. Hull, telegram to Grew, April 28, 1934, *FRUS, Japan*, 1:232.

37. Grew diary, April 28, 1934; Phillips diary, April 28, 1934; Hull, *Memoirs*, 1:279; Moffat diary, May 10, 1934.

38. Saito to Hull, *FRUS, Japan*, 1:232–33; ibid., pp. 233-36. Hornbeck told me: "People have failed to realize that the Japanese in the 1930s

wanted a 'hunting license' from the United States to overrun the area west of an arbitrarily drawn line to separate the Pacific into a Japanese and an American sphere" (interview, Jan. 3, 1966).

39. Hull, *Memoirs*, 1:281-82.

40. Grew, *Turbulent Era*, pp. 1265-66; Stanley K. Hornbeck, *Contemporary Politics in the Far East*, p. 355: "We should recognize this difference; the American Monroe Doctrine is defensive and all excluding; the Japanese Monroe Doctrine is aggressive and not self-excluding."

41. Dispatch 1102, "The Importance of American Naval Preparedness in Connection with the Situation in the Far East, Summary of the Situation," in Grew diary, Dec. 27, 1934. The department was favorably impressed with this dispatch; see ibid., Feb. 14, 1935.

42. Hull, *Memoirs*, 1:290-91.

43. Memorandum by the chief of the Division of Far Eastern Affairs, May 24, 1934, *FRUS, 1934*, 3:189-93.

44. Moffat diary, May 10, 1934.

45. Grew diary, Jan. 9, 26, 1935, Feb. 7, 1936.

46. See Phillips's reaction to fraudulent imitation of American toothpicks by the Japanese (Phillips diary, Feb. 20, 1935), and Hornbeck's reaction to the dumping of Japanese sun-goggles on the American market (letter to Francis Sayre, April 3, 1935, Hornbeck Papers, Hoover Institution).

47. Memorandum, "Policy of the United States in and with Regard to the Far East," Sept. 27, 1935, Hornbeck Papers, Hoover Institution.

48. Grew, *Turbulent Era*, pp. 1002-3.

49. See Grew to John A. MacMurray, Nov. 24, 1937, and attached memorandum by MacMurray, Nov. 1, 1935, "Developments affecting American Policy in the Far East," John Van Antwerp MacMurray Papers.

CHAPTER 5

1. Robert A. Divine, "Franklin D. Roosevelt and Collective Security, 1933," pp. 42-44, 59; Charles A. Beard, *American Foreign Policy in the Making*, p. 124; Basil Rauch, *Roosevelt from Munich to Pearl Harbor*, p. 23.

2. Divine, "Roosevelt and Collective Security," p. 42. See also Robert A. Divine, *The Illusion of Neutrality*, p. 56.

3. The background material in this chapter is based upon Robert H. Ferrell, *American Diplomacy in the Great Depression*, Chap. 12, and Divine, *Illusion of Neutrality*, Chap. 2. For an illuminating discussion of collective security and neutrality in the 1920s, see Charles De Benedetti, "The Origins of Neutrality Revision."

4. Henry L. Stimson and McGeorge Bundy, *On Active Service in Peace and War*, p. 233; Richard Current, *Secretary Stimson*, pp. 80-81.

5. Memorandum by the Division of Far Eastern Affairs, March 7, 1933, "Manchurian Situation, Proposed Embargo on Export of Arms, Bearing of

this Proposal, if Adopted and Acted upon Relations of the United States with Countries of the Far East," 893.113/1467; italics in original. See also "Manchurian Situation, Rumor that British Government Intends to Communicate with the Principal Powers on the Question of Embargo of Arms to the Far East," Stanley K. Hornbeck, Papers, Hoover Institution.

6. Stanley K. Hornbeck, "Manchuria Situation, Constant Factors for Consideration in Connection with Problem of American-Japanese Relations," March 14, 1933, Hornbeck Papers, Subject file, American-Japanese Relations.

7. Jay Pierrepont Moffat Diary, March 7, 1933; see also Memorandum, Division of Western European Affairs, March 9, 1933, 811.113/264.

8. Memorandum of Conversation between Mr. Green and Representative Tinkham, 11th District, Massachusetts, re: Arms Embargo Resolution, April 10, 1933, Hornbeck Papers, Subject file, Arms Embargo.

9. William R. Allen, "The International Trade Philosophy of Cordell Hull, 1907–1933," p. 102.

10. *Congressional Record,* 65th Cong., 3d sess., Feb. 21, 1919, vol. 57, pt. 4, p. 3955.

11. Allen, "International Trade Philosophy," p. 106.

12. Herbert Feis, *1933,* p. 98.

13. Nancy Harvison Hooker, ed., *The Moffat Papers,* pp. 92-93.

14. Moffat diary, March 6, 1933.

15. Davis, telegram 163 to Hull, April 16, 1933, *FRUS, 1933,* 1:92; telegram 164 to Hull, ibid., pp. 96-97 (italics added); telegram 165 to Hull, ibid., p. 98.

16. Apparently Hull was convinced by Moffat a month later that it was a mistake to link disarmament to the forthcoming economic conference. On May 14, 1933, Moffat wrote in his diary: "Then the Secretary came in and for the next hour the talk turned to the economic end of the picture. I told him that I thought that we had been making a great mistake in emphasizing that military disarmament was a prerequisite to the success of the Economic Conference. I did not think it would be possible to salvage the Disarmament Conference much longer. I figured that its failure might now react more adversely on the prospects of the London Conference than would have been the case had we not made the one appear dependent upon the other. The Secretary agreed and told us to adopt a tone that the two Conferences were equal and co-ordinate parts of the same problem."

17. "Memorandum of the Disarmament Situation," undated, Norman H. Davis Papers, File Box 21.

18. In this connection, Moffat noted, "A long telegram in twelve sections from Norman Davis, recommending what he considered the price we will have to pay for arms reduction in Europe. As he sees it, it will not be in terms of disarmament for us.... The cheapest price would be an arrangement not to interfere with a blockade against a *continental* aggressor provided we, on our independent judgment likewise agreed that she had violated her undertakings" (Moffat diary, April 17, 1933; italics in original).

19. Hull to Davis, April 25, 1933, *FRUS, 1933,* 1:116.

20. Moffat recorded in his diary on April 24, 1933, that "Bill Phillips and I were so out of sympathy with the draft instructions to Norman Davis that we went and saw the Secretary just as soon as he arrived in the morning. We pointed out that not only would acceptance of Part I of the British Plan involve us far deeper than at present, but pointed out the various deficiencies of the MacDonald Plan."

21. Davis, telegram to Hull, April 27, 1933, *FRUS, 1933,* 1:116.

22. Moffat observed: "They [Hugh Wilson and Davis] are clearly extremely unhappy at the President's whole-hearted acceptance of the MacDonald Plan and pointed out once again many ways in which it would not work to our immediate interests" (Moffat diary, May 4, 1933).

23. Department of State, *Press Releases,* May 27, 1933, pp. 387-92.

24. "Memorandum of a Conference held by Mr. Norman Davis for American Correspondents," Geneva, May 22, 1933, Davis Papers, File Box 22. At this point Davis may have been trying to alleviate American fears of involvement. The State Department in general, and Cordell Hull in particular, were sensitive to attacks made by the press (Hooker, ed., *Moffat Papers,* pp. 106, 108). The popular reaction against any form of involvement at this time was fierce. See Roland N. Stromberg, *Collective Security and American Foreign Policy,* p. 89. Discussions of isolationist sentiment can be found in Selig Adler, *The Isolationist Impulse;* Ray A. Billington, "The Origins of Middle Western Isolationism"; and Alexander DeConde, "The South and Isolationism."

25. Moffat raised two objections to Davis's speech: "It struck me that there were two places where the phraseology was dangerous, one promising to consult with machinery which might hereafter be set up. This seemed to me like signing a blank check. The other was a promise that our declaration would be attached to our instrument of ratification. This seemed like being-too specific as to procedure far too early in the game" (Moffat diary, May 23, 1933).

26. Ibid., May 31, 1933.

27. Ibid., Oct. 16, 1933.

28. *FRUS, 1933,* 1:277.

29. Divine, "Roosevelt and Collective Security," p. 56.

30. Memorandum, Jan. 23, 1934, Moffat Papers.

31. Moffat diary, March 31–April 1, April 5, 1934. In 1934, Davis's anxiety over the prospects of disarmament prompted him to advocate a more active role for the United States in collective security than he had advised previously. Moffat observed, "He [Norman Davis] is as convinced as ever that we should return to the disarmament venture. . . . It is like watching a war-horse when he smells the powder. I wish I could agree, but to my way of thinking it would be a greater mistake to return to active participation in general disarmament at the moment. Our whole energy should be centered on reaching a meeting of minds with the British on the specific ques-

tion of the Far Eastern and Naval situations in 1935. As a matter of fact, the President approved a telegram I had prepared commenting on a conversation between MacDonald and Atherton relative to the necessity of studying the potentialities of the situation if the treaty should go by the board" (ibid., Jan. 31, 1934).

32. Moffat diary, May 15, 17, 28, 1934.

33. Davis to Hull, Oct. 9, 1934, Davis Papers, File Box 37.

34. Divine interprets the State Department's attitude, specifically the views of Hull and Davis, differently. He argues, "The arms embargo resolution of 1933, intended as a springboard for American participation in collective security, became instead the last stand of the internationalists. In the next two years, other groups began to take over the arms embargo concept and turn it to quite different uses" (*Illusion of Neutrality*, p. 57).

CHAPTER 6

1. Robert A. Divine, *The Illusion of Neutrality*, chaps. 3 and 4. According to Manfred Jonas in *Isolationism in America, 1935-1941*, isolationists divided into roughly five groups: foreign-oriented, belligerent, timid, radical, and conservative. These categories are useful in describing public and congressional sentiment but do not apply to the State Department. By and large the department's attitude was the nineteenth-century one—maintaining a flexible but aloof attitude toward European politics—which later acceded to public and congressional pressure to adopt total noninvolvement ("insulationism" in my view).

2. Robert H. Ferrell, "The Peace Movement," pp. 91-92, 102. Ernest C. Bolt, Jr., *Ballots before Bullets*, notes that "public disillusionment with diplomats and a subsequent drive to 'establish popular control of foreign policy,' or socialized diplomacy, was an important characteristic of the period" (p. 133). See also Charles DeBenedetti, *The Peace Reform in American History*, chap. 6; and Charles Chatfield, *For Peace and Justice*, pp. 235-38.

3. *Congressional Record*. U.S. Senate, 74th Cong., 1st sess., Special Munitions Committee, Aug. 5, 1935, vol. 79, pt. 2, pp. 12461-65.

4. *Congressional Record*. U.S. Senate, 73d Cong., 2d sess., S. Res. 179, Feb. 8, 1934, vol. 78, pt. 2, p. 2153. The two standard works on Nye are Wayne S. Cole, *Gerald P. Nye and American Foreign Relations*, and John E. Wiltz, *In Search of Peace*.

5. Helmuth C. Engelbrecht and F. C. Hanighen, *Merchants of Death*, p. 8; George Seldes, *Iron, Blood, and Profits*, p. 327.

6. "Arms and the Men," p. 53.

7. Divine, *Illusion of Neutrality*, p. 66.

8. Ibid.

9. Charles Warren, "Troubles of a Neutral," pp. 378, 380-86.

10. Allen Dulles, "The Cost of Peace," pp. 567-68, 570, 575.

11. Wilson to Hull, March 21, 1934, Cordell Hull Papers, File Box 36.

12. Jay Pierrepont Moffat Dairy, April 12, 1934.

13. Divine, *Illusion of Neutrality,* p. 70.

14. Phillips diary, June 1, 1934.

15. Charles Warren, "A Memorandum on Some Problems on the Maintenance and Enforcement of Neutrality of the United States," Aug. 1934, 811.04418/28.

16. Phillips diary, Sept. 24, 1934.

17. Ibid., Dec. 14, 1934.

18. Moffat diary, Dec. 19, 1934.

19. Phillips diary, Jan. 9, 1935.

20. Cordell Hull, *The Memoirs of Cordell Hull,* 1:234.

21. Walter Millis, *Road to War,* p. 336.

22. Nye to Green, Feb. 20, 1935, *FRUS, 1935,* 1:316.

23. Hull, memorandum to Roosevelt, March 14, 1935, ibid., 1:318-20. See also Hull, memorandum to Roosevelt, March 14, 1935, ibid., 1:322-23.

24. Phillips diary, April 1, 1935.

25. Memorandum by the legal adviser, April 2, 1935, *FRUS, 1935,* 1:327-28.

26. Hull, draft memorandum to Roosevelt, April 10, 1935, 811.04418/42 1/2, National Archives.

27. Green to Moffat, April 10, 1935, 811.04418/42 1/2, National Archives.

28. *New York Times,* April 11, 1935, p. 3.

29. Hull, memorandum to Roosevelt, April 11, 1935, *FRUS, 1935,* 1:322.

30. *Congressional Record,* 74th Cong., 1st sess., S.J. 99 and S.J. 100, April 9, 1935, vol. 79, pt. 5, pp. 5286-87.

31. Ibid., H.R. 5529, April 6, 1935, pp. 5184-85.

32. Ibid., "American Neutrality Policy," Hearing before the House Committee on Foreign Affairs, 74th Cong., 1st sess., on H.R. 7125 and H.J. Res. 259, July 18 and July 30, 1935.

33. Ibid., S.J. Res. 120, May 7, 1935, pt. 7, p. 7042.

34. Ibid., June 6, 1935, pt. 8, pp. 8790-99.

35. Phillips to Hull, June 28, 1935, 811.04418/55, National Archives.

36. Green to Davis, July 8, 1935, Norman H. Davis Papers, File Box 26.

37. Phillips to Roosevelt, July 16, 1935, *FRUS, 1935,* 1:342.

38. Memorandum by Undersecretary Phillips, July 29, 1935, *FRUS, 1935,* 1:343-44.

39. Divine, *Illusion of Neutrality,* p. 101. Phillips recorded in his diary that in July 1935 Davis wanted the president to have freedom of action to place an embargo because of the promise he made at Geneva (Phillips diary, July 20, 1935). Charles Warren, on the other hand, believed strongly in the Johnson amendment that would apply an embargo to both parties (ibid., July 23, 1935).

40. Meeting of Phillips, Moore, and Davis with Senators Pittman and Connolly, July 25, 1935, reported in Phillips diary, July 25.

41. Hornbeck, memorandum, "Preventing War," Aug. 1, 1935, Hornbeck Papers, Subject File: "Neutrality, 1933-1935," Hoover Institution.

42. Hornbeck, memorandum, Aug. 21, 1935, ibid.

43. Phillips diary, July 20, 1935.

44. *New York Times,* Aug. 18, 1935, p. 7.

45. Green to Davis, Aug. 19, 1935, Davis Papers, File Box 26.

46. Divine, *Illusion of Neutrality,* p. 110.

47. *Congressional Record,* 74th Cong., 1st sess., Aug. 20, 1935, vol. 79, pt. 13, pp. 13775-79, 13783, 13787, 13795-97.

48. Divine, *Illusion of Neutrality,* pp. 112-13.

49. Phillips diary, Oct. 1, 1935; italics added.

50. Cordell Hull, "Neutrality Controversy."

51. Herbert Feis, *Seen from E. A.,* p. 222. See also Phillips diary, Aug. 8, 1935.

CHAPTER 7

1. Herbert Feis, *Seen from E.A.,* pp. 218, 260.

2. Cordell Hull, *The Memoirs of Cordell Hull,* 1:429.

3. Wilson to Hull, Oct. 5, 1935, *FRUS, 1935,* 1:664-65.

4. Hull, *Memoirs,* 1:429.

5. Stanley K. Hornbeck, memorandum, Oct. 3, 1935, Hornbeck Papers, Subject File: "Neutrality, 1933-1935," Hoover Institution; William Phillips Diary, Oct. 3, 1935.

6. Phillips diary, Oct. 3, 4, 1935; Feis, *Seen from E.A.,* p. 235; Robert A. Divine, *The Illusion of Neutrality,* p. 123.

7. Roosevelt, telegram to Hull, Oct. 5, 1935, *FRUS, 1935,* 1:797-98.

8. Hull, *Memoirs,* 1:429; Hull, telegram to Roosevelt, Oct. 5, 1935, *FRUS, 1935,* 1:798.

9. Roosevelt to Hull, Oct. 4, 1935, *FRUS, 1935,* 1:794.

10. Hull to Roosevelt, Oct. 5, 1935, ibid., p. 799.

11. Herbert Feis, memorandum, "Skeleton outline of the elements involved in the decision regarding possible American action in the trade field taken in connection with the Italo-Ethiopian dispute," Oct. 4, 1935, 765.84/1523 1/10.

12. Phillips diary, Oct. 7, 1935.

13. Divine, *Illusion of Neutrality,* p. 123; Feis, *Seen from E.A.,* p. 235.

14. Divine, *Illusion of Neutrality,* p. 125.

15. Department of State, *Press Releases,* Oct. 12, 1935, pp. 303-4.

16. Unsigned Memorandum, "American Economic and Financial Intercourse with the Belligerents," Oct. 16, 1935, 765.84/1523-1/2.

17. Breckinridge Long Diary, Nov. 2, 1935, File Box 4.

18. Phillips diary, Nov. 12, 1935. See also James C. Dunn, memorandum by the chief of the Western European Division, Nov. 5, 1935, *FRUS, 1935,* 1:855-57.

19. Phillips diary, Nov. 15, 1935.

20. For a different view of the "moral embargo," see Brice Harris, Jr., *The United States and the Italo-Ethiopian Crisis,* p. 93.

21. Phillips diary, Nov. 15, 1935; Long diary, Nov. 27, 1935.

22. Phillips diary, July 10, 1935.

23. Stanley K. Hornbeck, memorandum to the secretary of state, "Keeping Out of War," July 31, 1935, Hornbeck Papers, Subject file, "Neutrality, 1933-1935," Hoover Institution; memorandum from the Division of Far Eastern Affairs to the secretary of state, Sept. 26, 1935, 765.84/1493, National Archives.

24. Stanley K. Hornbeck, memorandum to the secretary of state, Sept. 28, 1935, Hornbeck Papers, Subject file, "Neutrality, 1933-1935," Hoover Institution.

25. Breckinridge Long to William S. Logan, Aug. 9, 1933, Long Papers, File Box 104; Long, undated memorandum, "Not Used File, B.L.," Long Papers, File Box 113.

26. Long diary, Sept. 11, 12, 18, 1935.

27. Cordell Hull, statement to the press by the secretary of state, Sept. 12, 1935, *FRUS, 1935,* 1:749; Hull, telegram to the chargé in the United Kingdom, Sept. 20, 1935, ibid., p. 837.

28. Memorandum, Division of Far Eastern Affairs to the undersecretary, Oct. 4, 1935, 765.84/1960.

29. Phillips diary, Oct. 9, 1935.

30. Hull, telegram to Wilson, Oct. 9, 1935, *FRUS, 1935,* 1:843.

31. Phillips diary, Oct. 9, 1935.

32. Hull, telegram to Consul Gilbert, Oct. 17, 1935, *FRUS, 1935,* 1:846-48; Department of State, *Press Releases,* Nov. 2, 1935, p. 337.

33. Phillips diary, Oct. 26, 1935; Long diary, Oct. 29, 1935.

34. Chargé in Ethiopia, Engert, telegram to the secretary of state, Oct. 30, 1935, *FRUS, 1935,* 1:776-77.

35. Hull, telegram to Engert, Oct. 31, 1935, ibid., pp. 777-78, 765.84/2215.

36. Phillips, telegram to Wilson, Nov. 4, 1935, ibid., p. 855, 765.84/2263. See also memorandum of a conversation between James Clement Dunn and Wilson in which the chief of the Western European Division stated: "In order that we may maintain our independent position in carrying out the policies we have adopted toward this situation, it is extremely important that there be no request to us at this stage for information with regard to any action we might take with regard to the shipment of any specific commodities. We feel sure you will make every effort to make our position clear in this regard"(Nov. 5, 1935, ibid., pp. 855-57).

37. Feis, *Seen from E.A.,* p. 307; Phillips diary, Nov. 25, 1935. Phillips noted: "This League postponement leaves us somewhat 'out on a limb' since

we have already included oil in our list of war materials which we are discouraging for shipment to the belligerents."

38. Long diary, Nov. 22, 1935; Long to Roosevelt, Nov. 29, 1935, Long Papers, File Box 114.

39. Oral communication from the British Embassy to the Department of State, Dec. 5, 1935, *FRUS, 1935,* 1:871; memorandum by the secretary of state, Dec. 7, 1935, ibid., p. 873.

40. Hornbeck, memorandum headed "Comment on Mr. Hackworth's memorandum on neutrality of December 27, 1937, Jan. 2, 1936, Hornbeck Papers, Subject file, "Neutrality, 1936," Hoover Institution.

41. Hull, memorandum, Department of State, the secretary, Jan. 17, 1937, Cordell Hull Papers, File Box 80-A.

42. Memorandum by the legal adviser, May 7, 1936, *FRUS, 1936,* 3:222-25; memorandum of the undersecretary, May 15, 1936, ibid., p. 234; memorandum by the chief of the division of Far Eastern Affairs, May 18, 1936, ibid., pp. 197-98.

43. Engert, telegram to Hull, June 5, 1936, ibid., pp. 205-6; Hull to Roosevelt, June 12, 1936, ibid., pp. 208-9; Hull, telegram to Engert, June 16, 1936, ibid., pp. 209-10; Engert, telegram to Hull, June 18, 1936, ibid., pp. 210-11; memorandum by the legal adviser, June 19, 1936, ibid., pp. 211-12.

44. Some department members, like Ambassador William E. Dodd, thought Roosevelt would never recognize Italian conquest in Ethiopia. See Registry number A8860/103/45, telegram from Sir E. Phills (Berlin), No. 331 (Savin), confidential, Nov. 6, 1936, Public Record Office.

CHAPTER 8

1. Dante A. Puzzo, *Spain and the Great Powers, 1936–1941,* p.v. An excellent study of American policy in Spain is Richard P. Traina, *American Diplomacy and the Spanish Civil War.*

2. Claude Bowers, *My Mission to Spain,* p. 414.

3. Norman J. Padelford, *International Law and Diplomacy in the Spanish Civil Strife,* pp. 174-75.

4. Hugh Thomas, *The Spanish Civil War,* p. 112.

5. By this time the communists had successfully infiltrated the anarchist and syndicalist parties; however, the Falange rose more rapidly than the communists. See F. Jay Taylor, *TheUnited States and the Spanish Civil War, 1936–1939,* chap. 1.

6. P. A. M. van der Esch, *Prelude to War,* chap. 1.

7. Ibid., p. 60.

8. Ambassador Straus to Hull, July 27, 1936, *FRUS, 1936,* 2:449, 852.00/2290.

9. Van der Esch, *Prelude to War,* p. 61; Puzzo, *Spain and the Great Powers,* p. 244; Thomas, *The Spanish Civil War,* pp. 614-15.

10. Padelford, *International Law,* p. 119.

11. In the diplomatic dispatches of the State Department there are numerous references to foreign intervention during the Spanish Civil War. See, for example: Ambassador Bowers to Hull, July 30, 1936, *FRUS, 1936,* 2:450, 852.00/2325; Ambassador Straus to Hull, July 31, 1936, ibid., p. 451, 852.00/2334; Chargé in the Soviet Union Henderson to Hull, Aug. 4, 1936, ibid., p. 461, 852.00/2395; Chargé in France Wilson to Hull, Aug. 6, 1936, ibid., p. 467, 852.00/2450; Vice Consul at Vigo Steward to Hull, Aug. 29, 1936, ibid., p. 517, 852.—/2877; Consul at Seville Bay to the acting secretary of state, Nov. 18, 1936, ibid., p. 558, 852.00/3796; Phillips to the acting secretary, Nov. 28, 1936, ibid., p. 582, 852.00/3913; Ambassador Dodd to the acting secretary, Dec. 29, 1936, ibid., p. 617, 852.00/4206, National Archives.

12. Taylor, *The United States and the Spanish Civil War,* chap. 4.

13. Bowers, *My Mission to Spain,* p. 414.

14. Claude Bowers, Introduction to Taylor, *The United States and the Spanish Civil War,* p. 19.

15. Claude Bowers to Cordell Hull, Sept. 23, 1936, Hull Papers.

16. Sumner Welles, *The Time for Decision,* p. 57.

17. Taylor, *The United States and the Spanish Civil War,* chap. 2.

18. Cordell Hull, *The Memoirs of Cordell Hull,* 1:481-84.

19. Taylor, *The United States and the Spanish Civil War,* chap. 2.

20. Hull, *Memoirs,* 1:476-77.

21. Phillips to all consulates in Spain, Aug. 7, 1936, *FRUS, 1936,* 2:471, italics added.

22. Stanley K. Hornbeck, note attached to a memorandum addressed to the secretary of state, Aug. 11, 1936, Hornbeck Papers, Subject file, "Neutrality—1936," Hoover Institution.

23. See Padelford, *International Law,* pp. 174-75.

24. Memorandum by the secretary of state, Aug. 4, 1936, *FRUS, 1936,* 2:457-58.

25. Memorandum by Acting Secretary Phillips, Aug.11, 1936, ibid., p. 478.

26. Moore to Hull, Dec. 5, 1936, 852.00/4007A, National Archives.

27. Department of State, *Press Releases,* Dec. 12, 1936, pp. 496-97.

28. Bowers to Hull, May 8, 1935, Hull Papers, File Box 38.

29. Puzzo, *Spain and the Great Powers,* p. 165.

30. Hull, *Memoirs,* 1:475.

31. Robert A. Friedlander, "Great Power Politics and the Spanish Civil War," p. 28.

32. Memorandum of a conversation with the Uruguayan minister by Undersecretary Phillips, Aug. 17, 1936, 852.00/2700, National Archives; Phillips to the Uruguayan minister, Aug. 20, 1936, *FRUS, 1936,* 2:498-99.

33. Bowers, telegram to Hull, Aug. 17, 1936, *FRUS, 1936,* 2:488; Phillips, telegram to Bowers, Aug. 17, 1936, ibid., p. 488.

34. Memorandum by the chief of the Division of Western Europe, Dunn, Dec. 5, 1936, ibid., pp. 489-590.

35. Memorandum by Dunn, Dec. 8, 1936, 852.00/4142, National Archives.

36. Memorandum by Dunn, Dec. 9, 1936, *FRUS, 1936,* 2:596. See also Moore to Roosevelt, Dec. 10, 1936, 852.00/4048A, in which the acting secretary told the president that Hull approved of the statement.

37. Department of State, *Press Releases,* Dec. 12, 1936, pp. 496-97; italics added.

38. Taylor, *The United States and the Spanish Civil War,* chap. 2.

39. One indication of Mexican support for the Loyalist cause was Mexico's refusal to participate in mediation efforts. On August 18, 1936, Ambassador Daniels wrote to Hull that the Mexican foreign minister opposed mediation in the Spanish conflict because the Mexican government was sympathetic to the Republican cause. Daniels attributed Mexico's sympathy to Mexico's fear of fascism. The ambassador also mentioned that the foreign minister expressed the hope that the Pan-American Conference at Buenos Aires would succeed and that in the future the United States would tie itself more closely to Latin America than to Europe. Apparently Daniels agreed with the foreign minister's observation because, he wrote Hull, "While necessarily absorbed in the European situation, is not our future more tied up with (this) Continent?" (Daniels to Hull, Aug. 18, 1936, Hull Papers, unnumbered File Box).

40. Daniels to Hull, Aug. 20, 1936, *FRUS, 1936,* 2:505-6.

41. Memorandum by Reed, Sept. 14, 1936, ibid., p. 530; memorandum by Reed, Sept. 15, 1936, ibid., p. 531.

42. Acting Secretary Moore to Chargé Boal, Dec. 31, 1936, ibid., pp. 624-25.

43. Department of State, *Press Releases,* Aug. 15, 1936, p. 152.

44. Stanley K. Hornbeck, memorandum headed "The Spanish Civil Conflict and the Problem of 'Nonintervention,' " Aug. 11, 1936, Hornbeck Papers, Subject file, "Neutrality—1936," Washington, D.C.

45. Stanley K. Hornbeck, memorandum headed "The Spanish Civil Conflict and the question of American Policy as regards Cooperation with Other Powers in Placing an Embargo on Sale and Export of Arms," Aug. 11, 1936, 852.00/2522.

46. Hull, *Memoirs,* 1:479.

47. Sumner Welles, *Our Foreign Policy and Peace,* p. 12.

48. Cordell Hull, *Our Foreign Relations and Our Foreign Policy,* p. 9.

49. Moore to Bullitt, Dec. 29, 1936, *FRUS, 1936,* 2:618-20.

CHAPTER 9

1. William W. Kauffman, "Two American Ambassadors," p. 654.

2. Interview with Stanley K. Hornbeck, in Howard Jablon, "Cordell Hull, the State Department, and the Foreign Policy of the First Roosevelt Administration, 1933–1936," Ph.D. diss, Rutgers, 1967, p. 248.

EPILOGUE

1. John McVikar Haight, Jr., "Franklin D. Roosevelt and a Naval Quarantine of Japan," p. 203.

2. Hans J. Morgenthau, *Politics among Nations,* pp. 3-15.

3. George F. Kennan, *American Diplomacy, 1900–1950,* pp. 74–90, 91-103.

Bibliography

Primary Sources

MANUSCRIPT COLLECTIONS

Carr, Wilbur J. Papers. Library of Congress, Washington, D.C.

Davis, Norman H. Papers. Library of Congress, Washington, D.C.

Grew, Joseph C. Diary and Papers. Houghton Library, Harvard University, Cambridge, Massachusetts.

Hornbeck, Stanley K. Papers. Hoover Institution, Stanford University, Palo Alto, California.

Hull, Cordell. Papers. Library of Congress, Washington, D.C.

Long, Breckinridge. Diary and Papers. Library of Congress, Washington, D.C.

MacMurray, John Van Antwerp. Papers. Princeton University Library, Princeton, New Jersey.

Moffat, Jay Pierrepont. Diary and Papers. Houghton Library, Harvard University, Cambridge, Massachusetts.

Moley, Raymond. Papers. Hoover Institution, Stanford University, Palo Alto, California.

Moore, R. Walton. Papers. Franklin D. Roosevelt Library, Hyde Park, New York.

National Archives. Record Group 59, General Records. Department of State, Washington, D.C.

Phillips, William. Diary. Houghton Library, Harvard University, Cambridge, Massachusetts.

Public Record Office. London, England.

Sayre, Francis B. Papers. Library of Congress, Washington, D.C.

Stimson, Henry. Diary and Papers. Sterling Memorial Library, Yale University, New Haven, Connecticut.

INTERVIEW

Hornbeck, Stanley K. January 3, 5, 6, 1966, Washington, D.C.

PERSONAL COMMUNICATIONS

Feis, Herbert. Letter to author, January 1966.
Hornbeck, Stanley K. Two letters to author, January 1966.
Phillips, William. One letter to author, February 1966.
Tittmann, Harold H. One letter to author, February 1966.

PUBLIC DOCUMENTS AND GOVERNMENT PUBLICATIONS

Congressional Record 75th Cong., 3d sess., 1938. Vol. 83, pt. 6. Washington, D.C.: U.S. Government Printing Office.
The Department of State Press Releases: 1933-36. Weekly Issues, nos. 171-222, 1933; 223-74, 1934; 275-326, 1935; 327-78, 1936. Washington, D.C.: U.S. Government Printing Office.
Foreign Relations of the United States, Diplomatic Papers, 1933. 5 vols. Vol. 1, 1950; vol. 2, 1949; vol. 3, 1949; vol. 4, 1950; vol. 5, 1952. Washington, D.C.: U.S. Government Printing Office.
Foreign Relations of the United States, Diplomatic Papers, 1934. 5 vols. Vol. 1, 1951; vol. 2, 1951; vol. 3, 1950; vol. 5, 1952. Washington, D.C.: U.S. Government Printing Office.
Foreign Relations of the United States, Diplomatic Papers, 1935. 4 vols. Vol. 1, 1953. Washington, D.C.: U.S. Government Printing Office.
Foreign Relations of the United States, Diplomatic Papers, 1936. 5 vols. Vol. 3, 1953; vol. 5, 1954. Washington, D.C. U.S. Government Printing Office.
Papers Relating to the Foreign Relations of the United States, Japan, 1931-41. 2 vols. Vol. 1, 1943. Washington, D.C.: U.S. Government Printing Office.
Foreign Relations of the United States, Diplomatic Papers, The Soviet Union, 1933-39. Vol. 1, 1952; vol. 2, 1952. Washington, D.C.: U.S. Government Printing Office, 1952. Hornbeck, Stanley K. *Principles of American Policy in Relation to the Far East.* Address before the Ninth Conference on the Cause and Cure of War, Washington, January 18, 1934. Washington, D.C.: U.S. Government Printing Office, 1934.

Hull, Cordell. *Our Foreign Relations and Our Foreign Policy*. Address before the Good Neighbor League, New York City, September 15, 1936. U.S. Department of State, Publication No. 925. Washington, D.C.: U.S. Government Printing Office, September, 1936.

——. *The Path to Recovery*. Address to the Members of the Associated Press, New York City, April 23, 1934. Washington, D.C.: U. S. Government Printing Office, 1934.

——. *Peace and War*. Address at Brown University, Providence, Rhode Island, June 15, 1936. Washington, D.C.: U.S. Government Printing Office, 1936.

——. *Some Aspects of American Foreign Policy*. Address before the Canadian Society of New York, New York City, February 16, 1935. Washington, D.C.: U.S. Government Printing Office, 1935.

——. *Some of the Results of the Montevideo Conference*. Address by the Honorable Cordell Hull, Secretary of State, before the National Press Club, Washington, February 10, 1934. Department of State, Conference Series, No. 18. Washington, D.C.: U.S. Government Printing Office, 1934.

Messersmith, George S. *Some Aspects of the Assistance Rendered by the Department of State and Its Foreign Service to American Business*. Address at the Convention of the National Foreign Trade Council, Cleveland, Ohio, November 3, 1937. Washington, D.C.: U.S. Government Printing Office, 1937.

Moore, R. Walton. *The Outlook for Peace*. Address at the Institute of Public Affairs, University of Virginia, Charlottesville, July 5, 1937. Washington, D.C.: U.S. Government Printing Office, 1937.

Phillips, William. *Current Activities of the Department of State*. Address before the American Acceptance Council, New York City, January 28, 1935. Washington, D.C.: U.S. Government Printing Office, 1935.

Sayre, Francis B. *The "Good Neighbor" Policy and Trade Agreements*. Address before the Institute of Citizenship, Emory University, Atlanta, Georgia, February 12, 1937. Washington, D.C.: U.S. Government Printing Office, 1937.

——. *The Protection of American Export Trade*. Being the course of lectures delivered at Westminster College, Fulton, Missouri, 1939. Chicago, Ill.: University of Chicago Press, 1940.

——. *Trade Policies and Peace*. Address before the Wharton School of Finance and Commerce, University of Pennsylvania,

Philadelphia, January 20, 1936. Washington, D.C.: U. S. Government Printing Office, 1936.

U.S. Congress. House Committee on Foreign Affairs. *Hearings before the Committee on Foreign Affairs: American Neutrality Policy.* 75th Cong., 1st sess., H. J. Res. 147, 1937.

Welles, Sumner. *Our Foreign Policy and Peace.* Address before the Foreign Policy Association, New York City, October 19, 1936. U.S. Department of State, Publication No. 946. Washington, D.C., October 1936.

———. *Present Aspects of World Peace.* Address before the Institute of Public Affairs, University of Virginia, Charlottesville, July 7, 1937. Washington, D.C.: U.S. Government Printing Office, 1937.

———. *The Trade-Agreements Program in our Inter-American Relations.* Address before the Bar Association of Baltimore City, Baltimore, Maryland, February 4, 1936. Washington, D.C.: U.S. Government Printing Office, 1936.

Secondary Sources

ARTICLES AND ESSAYS

Allen, William R. "The International Trade Philosophy of Cordell Hull, 1907-33." *American Economic Review,* 43 (March 1953): 101-16.

"Arms and the Men." *Fortune* 9, no. 8 (March 1934): 52-57, 113-26.

Benjamin, Jules R. "The New Deal, Cuba, and the Rise of a Global Foreign Economic Policy." *Business History Review* 51 (Spring 1977): 57-78.

Billington, Ray A. "The Origins of Middle Western Isolationism"; and *Political Science Quarterly* 60 (March 1945): 44-64.

Borg, Dorothy. "Notes on Roosevelt's Quarantine Speech." *Political Science Quarterly* 72 (1957): 405-33.

Buell, Raymond Leslie. "The New Deal and Liberia." *The New Republic* 76 (August 16, 1933): 17-19.

Cole, Wayne S. "American Entry into World War II: A Historiographical Appraisal." *Mississippi Valley Historical Review* 43 (1956-57): 395-617.

Cronon, F. David. "Interpreting the New Good Neighbor Policy: The Cuban Crisis of 1933." *Hispanic American Historical Review* 39 (1959): 538-67.

De Benedetti, Charles. "The Origins of Neutrality Revision: The American Plan of 1924." *The Historian* 5 (1972): 75-89.

De Conde, Alexander. "The South and Isolationism." *Journal of Southern History* 24 (August 1958): 332-46.

Divine, Robert A. "Franklin D. Roosevelt and Collective Security, 1933." *Mississippi Valley Historical Review* 48 (1961-62): 42-59.

Driggs, Don W. "The President as Chief Educator on Foreign Affairs." *Western Political Quarterly* 11 (December 1958): 813-19.

Drummond, Donald F. "Cordell Hull." In *An Uncertain Tradition: American Secretaries of State in the Twentieth Century,* edited by Norman A. Graebner, pp. 184-209. New York: McGraw-Hill, 1961.

DuBois, W. E. Burghardt. "Liberia, the League and the United States." *Foreign Affairs* 11 (July 1933): 682-95.

Duggan, Laurence. "Our Relations with the Other American Republics." *Annals of the American Academy of Political and Social Science* 198 (July 1938): 128-32.

Dulles, Allen. "The Cost of Peace." *Foreign Affairs* 12 (July 1934): 567-78.

Feis, Herbert. "Open Door at Home." *Foreign Affairs* 13 (July 1935): 600-11.

Ferrell, Robert H. "The Peace Movement." In *Isolation and Security,* edited by Alexander DeConde, pp. 82-106. Durham, N.C.: Duke University Press, 1957.

Friedlander, Robert A. "Great Power Politics and the Spanish Civil War: The First Phase." *The Historian* 28 (November 1965): 72-95.

Grady, Henry F. "The New Trade Policy of the United States." *Foreign Affairs* 14 (January 1936): 283-96.

Green, Joseph C. "Supervising the American Traffic in Arms." *Foreign Affairs* 15 (July 1937): 729-44.

Haight, John McVikar, Jr. "Franklin D. Roosevelt and a Naval Quarantine of Japan." *Pacific Historical Review* 40 (May 1971): 203-26.

Hallgren, Mauritz A. "Liberia in Shackles." *The Nation* 137 (August 16, 1933): 185-88.

Hull, Cordell. "Achievements of the Trade Agreements Policy after Five Years of Operation." *Congressional Digest* 18 (December 1939): 304-5.

———. "Foreign Policy of the United States." *Congressional Digest* 17 (August 1938): 215.

————. "Neutrality Controversy." *Congressional Digest* 15 (January 1936): 24-5.

Kauffmann, William W. "Two American Ambassadors, Bullitt and Kennedy." In *The Diplomats 1919-39,* 2 vols., edited by Gordon A. Craig and Felix Gilbert, 2:649-81. Princeton: Princeton University Press, 1963.

Repko, Allen F. "The Failure of Reciprocal Trade: United States-Germany Commercial Rivalry in Brazil." *Mid-America* 60 (January 1978): 3-21.

Rosen, Elliot A. "Intranationalism vs. Internationalism: The Interregnum Struggle for the Sanctity of the New Deal." *Political Science Quarterly* 81 (June 1966): 274-97.

Savelle, Max. "The International Approach to Early Anglo American History, 1492-1763." In *The Reinterpretation of Early American History,* edited by Ray Allen Billington, pp. 201-31. San Marino: Huntington Library, 1966.

Schlesinger, Arthur M., Jr. "Roosevelt and His Detractors." In *Understanding the American History and Its Interpretation,* edited by Edward N. Saveth, pp. 514-28. Boston: Little, Brown, 1954.

Thomson, James C., Jr. "The Role of the Department of State." In *Pearl Harbor as History,* edited by Dorothy Borg and Shumpei Okamoto, 81-106. New York: Columbia University Press, 1973.

Varg, Paul A. "The Economic Side of the Good Neighbor Policy: The Reciprocal Trade Program and South America." *Pacific Historical Review* 45 (February 1976): 47-71.

Warren, Charles. "Troubles of a Neutral." *Foreign Affairs* 12 (April 1934): 377-94.

Welles, Sumner. "New Era in Pan American Relations." *Foreign Affairs* 15 (April 1937): 443-54.

Wilson, Joan H. "American Business and the Recognition of the Soviet Union." *Social Science Quarterly* 52 (September 1981): 349-65.

BOOKS

Adler, Selig. *The Isolationist Impulse.* New York: Abelard-Schuman, 1957.

Allison, Graham T. *Essence of Decision: Explaining the Cuban Missile Crisis.* Boston: Little, Brown, 1971.

Beard, Charles A. *American Foreign Policy in the Making.* New Haven: Yale University Press, 1946.

Berle, Adolf A. *Latin America Diplomacy and Reality.* New York: Harper & Row, 1962.

Bixler, Raymond W. *The Foreign Policy of the United States in Liberia.* New York: Pageant Press, 1957.

Blum, John Morton. *From the Morgenthau Diaries: Years of Crisis, 1928-1938.* Boston: Houghton Mifflin, 1959.

Bolt, Ernest C. Jr. *Ballots before Bullets, The War Referendum Approach to Peace in America, 1914-1941.* Charlottesville: University Press of Virginia, 1977.

Borg, Dorothy. *The United States and the Far Eastern Crisis of 1933-1938: From the Manchurian Incident through the Initial Stage of the Undeclared Sino-Japanese War.* Cambridge: Harvard University Press, 1964.

Borg, Dorothy, and Shumpei Okamoto, eds. *Pearl Harbor as History: Japanese-American Relations, 1931-1941.* New York: Columbia University Press, 1973.

Bowers, Claude G. *My Mission to Spain: Watching the Rehearsal for World War II.* New York: Simon and Schuster, 1954.

Browder, Robert Paul. *The Origins of Soviet-American Diplomacy.* Princeton: Princeton University Press, 1953.

Bullitt, Orville H., ed. *For the President: Personal and Secret Correspondence betweeen Franklin D. Roosevelt and William C. Bullitt.* Boston: Houghton Mifflin, 1972.

Burns, James MacGregor. *Roosevelt: The Lion and the Fox.* New York: Harcourt, Brace, 1956.

Chatfield, Charles. *For Peace and Justice, Pacifism in America 1914-1941.* Knoxville: University of Tennessee Press, 1941.

Current, Richard. *Secretary Stimson, A Study in Statecraft.* New Brunswick, N.J.: Rutgers University Press, 1954.

Dahl, Robert A. *Congress and Foreign Policy.* New York: Harcourt, Brace, 1950.

Dallek, Robert. *Franklin D. Roosevelt and American Foreign Policy, 1932-1945.* New York: Oxford University Press, 1979.

DeBenedetti, Charles. *The Peace Reform in American History.* Bloomington, In., 1980.

DeConde, Alexander. *Isolation and Security.* Durham, N.C., 1957.

DeSantis, Hugh. *The Diplomacy of Silence.* Chicago: University of Chicago Press, 1980.

Divine, Robert A. *The Illusion of Neutrality.* Chicago: University of Chicago Press, 1962.

Elder, Robert Ellsworth. *The Policy Machine: The Department of State and American Foreign Policy.* Syracuse: Syracuse University Press, 1960.

Engelbrecht, Helmuth C. and F. C. Hanighen. *Merchants of Death: A Study of the International Armaments Industry.* New York: Dodd, Mead, 1934.

Farnsworth, Beatrice. *William C. Bullitt and the Soviet Union.* Bloomington: Indiana University Press, 1967.

Feis, Herbert. *1933: Characters in Crisis.* Boston: Little, Brown, 1966.

―――. *Seen from E. A.: Three International Episodes.* New York: Alfred A. Knopf, 1947.

Ferrell, Robert H. *American Diplomacy in the Great Depression.* New Haven: Yale University Press, 1957.

Frankel, Charles. *Morality and United States Foreign Policy.* New York: Foreign Policy Association, 1975.

Freidel, Frank. *Franklin D. Roosevelt: Launching the New Deal.* Boston: Little, Brown, 1973.

Gardner, Lloyd C. *Economic Aspects of New Deal Diplomacy.* Madison: University of Wisconsin Press, 1964.

Gellman, Irwin F. *Roosevelt and Batista: Good Neighbor Diplomacy in Cuba, 1933-1945.* Albuquerque: University of New Mexico Press, 1973.

Geyl, Pieter. *Debates with Historians.* New York: Philosophical Library, 1956.

Grew, Joseph C. *Turbulent Era: A Diplomatic Record of Forty Years, 1904-1945.* Edited by Walter Johnson, assisted by Nancy Harvison Hooker. Boston: Houghton Mifflin, 1952.

Guttmann, Allen. *The Wound in the Heart: America and the Spanish Civil War.* New York: Free Press, 1962.

Harris, Brice, Jr. *The United States and the Italo-Ethiopian Crisis.* Stanford: Stanford University Press, 1964.

Hooker, Nancy Harvison, ed. *The Moffat Papers: Selections from the Diplomatic Journals of Jay Pierrepont Moffat, 1919-1943.* Cambridge: Harvard University Press, 1956.

Hornbeck, Stanley K. *Contemporary Politics in the Far East.* New York: D. Appleton, 1916.

―――. *The United States and the Far East: Certain Fundamentals of Policy.* Boston: World Peace Foundation, 1942.

Hull, Cordell. *The Memoirs of Cordell Hull.* 2 vols. New York: Macmillan, 1948.

Ickes, Harold L. *The Secret Diary of Harold L. Ickes: The First Thousand Days, 1933-1936.* 2 vols. New York: Simon and Schuster, 1953.

Ilchman, Warren Frederick. *Professional Diplomacy in the United States, 1779-1939: A Study in Administrative History.* Chicago: University of Chicago Press, 1961.

Jonas, Manfred. *Isolationism in America, 1935-1941.* Ithaca, N.Y.: Cornell University Press.

Kennan, George F. *American Diplomacy,* 1900-1950. Chicago: University of Chicago Press, 1951.

Kottman, Richard N. *Reciprocity and the North Atlantic Triangle, 1932-1938.* Ithaca: Cornell University Press, 1968.

Leuchtenburg, William E. *Franklin D. Roosevelt and the New Deal.* New York: Harper & Row, Torchbooks, 1963.

Millis, Walter. *Road to War: America, 1914-1917.* Boston: Houghton Mifflin, 1935.

Moley, Raymond. *After Seven Years.* New York: Harper & Brothers, 1939.

Morgenthau, Hans J. *Politics among Nations.* 5th edition. New York: Alfred A. Knopf, 1973.

Nixon, Edgar B., ed. *Franklin D. Roosevelt and Foreign Affairs.* 3 vols. Cambridge: The Belknap Press of Harvard University Press, 1969.

Padelford, Norman J. *International Law and Diplomacy in the Spanish Civil Strife.* New York: Macmillan, 1939.

Phillips, William. *Ventures in Diplomacy.* Boston: Beacon Press, 1952.

Pratt, Julius. *Cordell Hull.* New York: Cooper Square Publishers, 1964.

Puzzo, Dante A. *Spain and the Great Powers, 1936-1941.* New York: Columbia University Press, 1962.

Rappaport, Armin. *Henry L. Stimson and Japan, 1931-1933.* Chicago: University of Chicago Press, 1963.

Rauch, Basil. *Roosevelt from Munich to Pearl Harbor.* New York: Creative Age Press, 1950.

Sayre, Francis B. *Glad Adventure.* New York: Macmillan, 1957.

Seldes, George. *Iron, Blood, and Profits. An Exposure of the World-wide Munitions Racket.* New York and London, 1934.

Smith, Robert F. *The United States and Cuba, Business and Diplomacy, 1917-1960.* New York: Bookman Associates, 1960.

Snyder, Richard C., and Edgar S. Furniss, Jr. *American Foreign Policy: Formulation, Principles and Programs.* New York: Rinehart, 1954.

Stimson, Henry L. *The Far Eastern Crisis, Recollections and Observations.* New York: Harper, 1936.

—— and McGeorge Bundy, *On Active Service in Peace and War.* New York: Harper, 1947.

Stromberg, Roland N. *Collective Security and American Foreign Policy.* New York, 1963.

Taylor, F. Jay. *The United States and the Spanish Civil War, 1936-1939.* New York, 1956.

Thomas, Hugh. *The Spanish Civil War.* London: Eyre & Spottiswoode, 1961.

Traina, Richard P. *American Diplomacy and the Spanish Civil War.* Bloomington: Indiana University Press, 1968.

Tugwell, Rexford G. *The Democratic Roosevelt: A Biography of Franklin D. Roosevelt.* Garden City, N.Y.: Doubleday, 1957.

Van Alstyne, R. W. *The Rising American Empire.* Oxford: Basil Blackwell, 1960.

van der Esch, P.A.M. *Prelude to War: The International Repercussions of the Spanish Civil War, 1936-1939.* The Hague: Nijhoff, 1951.

Weil, Martin. *A Pretty Good Club: The Founding Fathers of the U.S. Foreign Service.* New York: Norton, 1978.

Weinberg, Albert K. *Manifest Destiny: A Study of Nationalist Expansionism in American History.* Baltimore: Johns Hopkins University Press, 1935.

Welles, Sumner. *The Time for Decision.* New York: Harper & Brothers, 1944.

Williams, William Appleman. *American-Russian Relations, 1781-1947.* New York: Rinehart, 1952.

The Tragedy of American Diplomacy. Revised edition. New York: Dell, 1962.

Wilson, Joan Hoff. *Ideology and Economics: U.S. Relations with the Soviet Union, 1918-1933.* Columbia: University of Missouri Press, 1974.

Wiltz, John E. *In Search of Peace: The Senate Munitions Inquiry, 1934-36.* Baton Rouge: Louisiana State University Press, 1963.

Wood, Bryce. *The Making of the Good Neighbor Policy.* New York: Columbia University Press, 1961.

Yergen, Daniel. *Shattered Peace: The Origins of the Cold War and the National Security State.* Boston: Houghton Mifflin, 1977.

Index